"THOUGH YOUR SINS BE AS SCARLET"

"THOUGH YOUR SINS
BE AS SCARLET"

BRENT L. TOP

Bookcraft
Salt Lake City, Utah

Library of Congress Catalog Card Number: 89–85674

ISBN 0–88494–713–0

First Printing, 1989

Printed in the United States of America

*Though your sins
be as scarlet,
they shall be
as white as snow;
though they be
red like crimson,
they shall be as wool.*

—Isaiah 1:18

Contents

Preface

"Say nothing but repentance unto this generation," commanded the Lord through the Prophet Joseph Smith (D&C 6:9). To the early missionaries and leaders of the Restoration the Lord would again declare "that the thing which will be of the most worth unto you will be to declare repentance unto this people, that you may bring souls unto me, that you may rest with them in the kingdom of my Father" (D&C 15:6). Repentance is the message of "most worth" because it is the crux of the gospel message.

> And this is the gospel, the glad tidings . . .
> That he came into the world, even Jesus, to be crucified for the world, and to bear the sins of the world, and to sanctify the world, and to cleanse it from all unrighteousness;
> That through him all might be saved (D&C 76:40–42).

This is the glorious, hopeful, joyful message we must declare to all the world, the "good tidings of great joy, which shall be to all people" (Luke 2:10). We must proclaim that the gift of repentance is made available to all by virtue of the infinite and eternal sacrifice of the Son of God and through the exercise of "faith unto repentance" (see Alma 34:14–16). Perhaps no other doctrine needs to be studied, understood, and applied more today, for it gives life and meaning to all other doctrines and principles of the gospel. "We believe in preaching the doctrine of repentance in all the world," the Prophet Joseph Smith stated. "But we discover, in order to be benefitted by the doctrine of repentance, we must believe in obtaining the remission of sins." (*History of the Church,* 2:256.) In other words, in order to fulfill the Lord's charge to "cry repentance unto this people" (D&C 18:14) we must not only *understand* the doctrine of repentance but we must also *apply* the principle in our own lives — tasting personally of the sweetness of a remission of sins.

Through years of teaching and counseling in my responsibilities as both a religious educator and a bishop, I have gained greater insights into this most vital doctrine. I have seen many who, though they have read the scriptures and have been "active" in the Church, seem to lack a fundamental understanding of the true nature of repentance. Some approach repentance almost mechanically — emphasizing "steps" of repentance without acknowledging the spiritual power that gives meaning to those components. Others approach it with fear and trepidation, having no feeling for the goodness of God's grace and love. Some, through an overwhelming sense of unworthiness, make repentance more difficult and demanding than it really is, while others, through self-justification or doctrinal distortion, attempt to make it easier than it is. Still others, downtrodden in deep despair, feel that they are beyond the redemptive rehabilitation of repentance. However, when we begin to sense the spiritual nature of repentance and understand the true doctrine as taught in the scriptures and by the living prophets, we can overcome such roadblocks to repentance.

It is my desire to share some of the insights I have gained from studying the scriptures, from counseling with others, from personal experience, and from the promptings of the Spirit. I hope that two important objectives will be met by this book. First, I hope that the reader will gain increased knowledge of the doctrine of repentance—an awakened awareness of the scriptural and prophetic teachings and an enhanced understanding of its importance in the plan of salvation. Second, and most important, it is my goal to lift readers to a higher sense of hope in Christ and to inspire all of us to "apply the atoning blood of Christ that we may receive forgiveness of our sins, and our hearts may be purified" (Mosiah 4:2). This twofold objective—*knowing* and *applying* the doctrine of repentance—will be needed constantly by each of us as we struggle through mortality. It is also my hope that an increased understanding of this doctrine will instruct, enlighten, and inspire those who teach and counsel others.

In addition to instruction, may this book likewise be an invitation. May the principles taught herein beckon all—especially those whose hearts are heavy and whose souls are sick with sin—to come unto him whose "yoke is easy" and whose "burden is light."

> To those who yearn for peace, we announce that it may be found with the Prince of Peace. Even in these tumultuous times the individual who turns to Christ can find the inner peace that surpasses understanding. . . . To those burdened and sorrowing with guilt, we offer hope. Your Redeemer loves you with a perfect love. He died to pay for the sins of all who truly repent and follow the course He prescribed. "Though your sins be as scarlet, they shall be as white as snow," He promised. (Isaiah 1:18.) Accept the healing of spirit that He alone can give. ("First Presidency Christmas Message," *Church News*, 15 December 1985, p. 3.)

1

"There Is No Peace to the Wicked"

On one occasion my wife and I had the opportunity to travel in the Middle East for several weeks with a group of religious educators from the Church Educational System. During our visit to Egypt we experienced some feelings that we will not forget. It was there that many of us American tourists had our first encounter with the conditions of poverty and uncleanliness that prevail in some less fortunate countries. The accommodations did not include the conveniences of sanitation and privacy to which we were accustomed. Though precautions were taken with food and drink, a few in the group still became ill from organisms which were not "at home" in their American digestive systems. Complicating these conditions was the extraordinary heat of an unusually hot, dry, and dusty Egyptian summer.

While in Luxor we avoided the midday inferno by touring early in the mornings and later in the afternoons and evenings. However, we were still exposed to intense heat. To visit the tombs of the ancient pharaohs required considerable walking along dusty trails. The physical exertion and strain of the day's activities in the unbearable desert heat soon left us sweaty, stinky, grimy, grouchy, and exhausted. At the conclusion of a visit to any particular site, there was often a hurried procession to the oasis-like comfort of the air-conditioned tour buses. Not infrequently, however, the buses would overheat and the air-conditioning would fail to operate.

After one particularly long day of this "torture" with no chance to bathe, change, or freshen up, we boarded a late-night train for a return trip to Cairo. We were cramped in hot and stuffy Pullman quarters in the old Luxor train, which seemed to have square wheels as it bumped and bounced along. It was futile to attempt to sleep during the fourteen-hour trip. The commingling odors of dirty and sweaty travelers, primitive sanitation facilities, and the unfamiliar aromas of Middle Eastern foods being served in the dining car now added queasiness to our discomfiture. Oh, how we longed to return to the comforts of our four-star Swiss hotel in Cairo!

There was a great sense of anticipation as we loaded the waiting buses at the Cairo rail station. There were hopeful comments about showers and shampoos, clean clothes and bedding. But it was not to be—at least not yet. Another full day of touring was required before we could return to the comforts of our hotel rooms. I can't remember ever feeling so dirty, so fatigued, so uncomfortable, and so hungry for a familiar meal.

These discomforts were not merely physical but also emotional. I did not want to go another mile, see another ancient site, or discover another important historical insight. I didn't want to get off the bus. I didn't even want to associate with my friends and colleagues. I knew that I might never be able to visit these places again, yet all I cared about was getting back to the hotel. I just wanted to be clean. It seemed like the longest day of my life as I counted the hours, minutes, and even seconds until the bus finally arrived at our hotel.

Never before had a shower, a shampoo, and a clean shave felt so exquisite. Simple things so often overlooked at home had never been enjoyed more—a cool room in the heat of the summer, clean water, clean sheets, a comfortable bed, and a simple but delicious meal. It felt so good to be clean. It felt so good to be able to rest. It felt so good to be, in a small way, at peace.

As I pondered the stark contrast of "before" and "after" feelings associated with this experience, I was led to compare the physical feelings of distress I had experienced to the spiritual side-effects of sin. I had experienced in my own life the feelings of uneasiness, pain, filthiness, and stress which result from sin and which are just as real and discomforting as those I felt in the summer heat and primitive conditions of Egypt. Because of this graphic object lesson, I suddenly understood more profoundly than ever before the significance of Isaiah's words: "But the wicked are like the troubled sea, when it cannot rest, whose waters cast up mire and dirt. There is no peace, saith my God, to the wicked." (Isaiah 57:19–21.)

President Harold B. Lee once stated, "The heaviest burden that anyone can carry in life is the burden of sin." Each of us has borne and continues to bear that burden to some degree or another. President Thomas S. Monson, illustrating how these burdens can weigh us down, brought to our attention a comparison of sins to barnacles that attach themselves to the hulls of ships.

> Ship captains . . . know that as their ships travel the seas, a curious salt water shellfish called a barnacle fastens itself to the hull and stays there for the rest of its life, surrounding itself with a rock-like shell. As more and more barnacles attach themselves, they increase the ship's drag, slow its progress, decrease its efficiency.
>
> Periodically, the ship must go into dry dock, where with great effort the barnacles are chiseled or scraped off. It's a difficult, expensive process that ties up the ship for days. . . .
>
> Sins are like those barnacles. Hardly anyone goes through life without picking up some. They increase the drag, slow our progress, decrease our efficiency. Unrepented, building up one on another, they can eventually sink us.[1]

The preacher in Ecclesiastes declared, "For there is not a just man upon the earth, that doeth good, and sinneth not" (Ecclesiastes 7:20). The Apostle Paul reminds us that "all have sinned, and come short of the glory of God" (Romans 3:23). These sentiments are also echoed in the warning of the beloved Apostle, John. "If we say that we have no sin," he wrote, "we deceive ourselves, and the truth is not in us" (1 John 1:8). Each of us has sinned, and though the nature of our sins and the burdens of guilt may vary, we all are subject to inspired pronouncements of the scriptures:

For I the Lord cannot look upon sin with the least degree of allowance (D&C 1:31).

But behold, I say unto you, the kingdom of God is not filthy, and there cannot any unclean thing enter into the kingdom of God (1 Nephi 15:34).

The wicked man travaileth with pain all his days (Job 15:20).

The Lord is known by the judgment which he executeth: the wicked is snared in the work of his own hands. . . . The wicked shall be turned into hell. (Psalm 9:16–17.)

But behold, an awful death cometh upon the wicked; for they die as to things pertaining to things of righteousness; for they are unclean, and no unclean thing can inherit the kingdom of God; but they are cast out, and consigned to partake of the fruits of their labors or their works, which have been evil; and they drink the dregs of a bitter cup (Alma 40:26).

The wrath of God shall be poured out upon the wicked without measure (D&C 1:9).

For, behold, the day cometh that . . . all the proud, yea, and all that do wickedly, shall be stubble; and the day that cometh shall burn them up, saith the Lord of hosts, that it shall leave them neither root nor branch (D&C 133:64; Malachi 4:1).

These and many other scriptural pronouncements remind us of the spiritual estrangement that inevitably occurs when we sin. They also warn us of the painful consequences awaiting those who willfully rebel against God and his laws. Who among us has not felt the fear that comes from acknowledging the justice of God's pronouncements and indictments against our evil ways? Who among us has not tasted the bitterness of that cup? Who among us has not felt the spiritual and emotional turmoil of the soul, like unto a "troubled sea" that "cannot rest"? Who among us has not experienced feelings similar to those described in the Book of Mormon by Alma?

> But I was racked with eternal torment, for my soul was harrowed up to the greatest degree and racked with all my sins.
>
> Yea, I did remember all my sins and iniquities, for which I was tormented with the pains of hell; yea, I saw that I had rebelled against my God, and that I had not kept his holy commandments. . . . Yea, and in fine so great had been my iniquities, that the very thought of coming into the presence of my God did rack my soul with inexpressible horror.
>
> Oh, thought I, that I could be banished and become extinct both soul and body, that I might not be brought to stand in the presence of my God, to be judged of my deeds. . . . I [was] racked, even with the pains of a damned soul. (Alma 36:12–16.)

Though our sins and circumstances differ, there is a universality in Alma's anguish. Each of us could describe similar painful emotions resulting from our own disobedience. We have learned through personal experience that sin destroys our self-esteem, undermines our faith, and leads to hopelessness and despair. "And if ye have no hope," wrote Moroni, "ye must needs be in despair; and despair cometh because of iniquity" (Moroni 10:22).

The burden of sin also creates a feeling of worthlessness as well as unworthiness. It often makes us feel that we can do nothing right. Our sense of shame falsely makes us feel that we are unworthy to approach our Father in Heaven in worship or in prayer. This further estranges us from our most important advocate and ally. "There is no loneliness so great, so absolute, so utterly complete," wrote Elder Richard L. Evans, "as the loneliness of a man who cannot call upon his God."[2]

Sinning brings a sense of loneliness even when we are surrounded by others. Job was told that "the light of the wicked shall be put out, and the spark of his fire shall not shine. The light shall be dark in his tabernacle, and his candle shall be put out with him." (Job 18:5–6.) There is indeed a spiritual darkness caused by sin. The Spirit of the Lord is grieved and withdrawn, and we are left alone—without the comfort, enlightenment, and inspiration of the Holy Ghost. There is no greater emptiness than to be void of the Spirit of the Lord.

Sometimes burdens of sin and guilt inflict physical maladies and ailments. Sinning can indeed make us sick, as evidenced by the description of the wicked Zeezrom who "lay sick at Sidom, with a burning fever, which was caused by the great tribulations of his mind on account of his wickedness. . . . [He was] sick, being very low with a burning fever; and his mind also was exceedingly sore because of his iniquities." (Alma 15:3, 5.) Discouragement, depression, discomfort, and distress often envelop us on account of our own iniquities and induce physical as well as spiritual sickness. This phenomenon was pointed out by Elder Boyd K. Packer of the Quorum of the Twelve in the October 1977 General Conference:

> I recently asked a doctor of family medicine how much of his time was devoted purely to correcting physical disorders. He has a large practice, and after thoughtfully considering, he answered, "Not more than 20 percent. The rest of the time I seem to be working on problems that very much affect the physical well-being of my patients but do not originate in the body.
>
> "These physical disorders," the doctor concluded, "are merely symptoms of some other kind of trouble."
>
> In recent generations one after another of the major diseases has yielded to control or cure. Some very

major ones still remain, but we now seem able to do something about most of them. . . .

There is another part of us, not so tangible, but quite as real as our physical body. This intangible part of us is described as mind, emotion, intellect, temperament, and many other things. Very seldom is it described as spiritual.

But there is a *spirit* in man; to ignore it is to ignore reality. *There are spiritual disorders, too, and spiritual diseases that can cause intense suffering.*

The body and the spirit of man are bound together. Often, very often, when there are disorders, it is very difficult to tell which is which.[3]

All too often accompanying our sin-induced spiritual sickness is the added discomfort of deception—of hiding a "dark secret." Many of us have felt that sense of hypocrisy that comes from knowing that our life does not reflect our professed ideals. One student who had cheated on a test in school described an audible voice speaking to his soul each time he attempted to pray or bless the sacrament. It whispered, "You're a liar! You're a cheat! You're a hypocrite!" While teaching seminary in Arizona I had an experience that taught me this principle in a startling way.

My wife and I had planned a weekend excursion to the temple in Mesa. I worked feverishly making mimeographed copies for my next seminary lesson, finishing just as my wife drove up. We made the three-hour trip to the temple and hurried into an endowment session totally unaware that anything was wrong. To my horror, as I raised my arm during the ceremony I noticed a big dark ink spot on the sleeve of my white shirt. I had inadvertently spilled black ink on my arm as I was making copies at the seminary building. Now I felt that everyone in the temple session could see the unsightly stain on my shirt. All were clothed in white, symbolic of personal purity, and yet there I stood in the midst of them with a hideous black blotch, conspicuous in its contrast to the white robes surrounding me. I was embarrassed and ashamed and desired to disappear. It was only an ink spot, but I felt unworthy.

Somehow I got through that humiliating experience, but I think I now better understand what the awful state of the wicked will be when their very real stains of sin are made painfully evident to all. "The rebellious shall be pierced with much sorrow; for their iniquities shall be spoken upon the housetops, and their secret acts shall be revealed" (D&C 1:3). Nephi likewise declared: "There is nothing which is secret save it shall be revealed; there is no work of darkness save it shall be made manifest in the light" (2 Nephi 30:17). In modern revelation the Lord has made it clear that he will "reveal the secret acts of men, and the thoughts and intents of their hearts" (D&C 88:109). We cannot hide our sins from the Lord, nor can we ultimately deceive our friends and family. Alma declared that "our words will condemn us, yea, all our works will condemn us; we shall not be found spotless; and our thoughts will also condemn us; and in this awful state we shall not dare to look up to our God; and we would fain be glad if we could command the rocks and the mountains to fall upon us to hide us from his presence" (Alma 12:14). The fear that our evil acts will be made public adds to the agony of sin.

When we are weighted down with the burdens of sin our souls are truly like the river of filthy waters (see 1 Nephi 15:26–30), made turbulent by the constant churning of guilt and shame. It seems as though there is no relief from the despair and the discouragement and the horror of hypocrisy. Even Alma's graphic description of his agony does not fully capture the unquenchable emotional, spiritual, and mental "fire" that burns within a sinner's soul. King Benjamin declared that this fire comes to man because "the demands of divine justice do awaken his immortal soul to a lively sense of his own guilt, which doth cause him to shrink from the presence of the Lord, and doth fill his breast with guilt, and pain, and anguish, which is like an unquenchable fire, whose flame ascendeth up forever and ever" (Mosiah 2:38).

Such torment and weight is real. David eloquently and ruefully recorded in psalm his perceptions of the "unquenchable fire" of his iniquities:

O Lord, rebuke me not in thy wrath: neither chasten me in thy hot displeasure.

For thine arrows stick fast in me, and thy hand presseth me sore.

There is no soundness in my flesh because of thine anger; neither is there any rest in my bones because of my sin.

For mine iniquities are gone over mine head: as an heavy burden they are too heavy for me.

My wounds stink and are corrupt because of my foolishness.

I am troubled; I am bowed down greatly; I go mourning all the day long.

For my loins are filled with a loathsome disease: and there is no soundness in my flesh.

I am feeble and sore broken: I have roared by reason of the disquietness of my heart.

Lord, all my desire is before thee; and my groaning is not hid from thee.

My heart panteth, my strength faileth me: as for the light of mine eyes, it also is gone from me.

My lovers and my friends stand aloof from my sore; and my kinsmen stand afar off. . . .

For I am ready to halt, and my sorrow is continually before me.

For I will declare mine iniquity; I will be sorry for my sin. (Psalm 38:1–11, 17–18.)

One cannot help but be moved with pity and compassion by the poignant pleadings and anguished accounts of Alma and David. Each of us can identify to some extent with their misery. From our own suffering and sorrow for sin come such soul-searching questions as "What if this burden of sin and shame can never be lifted?" and "What if I must feel 'eternal torment' and the 'pains of hell' forever?" Surely such thoughts strike within us a feeling described by Alma as "inexpressible horror."

Such would have been the case without the loving intercession of our Savior, Jesus Christ. Without the "infinite atonement," not only would we suffer the pains of hell and carry the burdens of sin in mortality but also ultimately "our spirits must have become like unto [the devil], and we become devils, angels to a devil, to be shut out from the presence of our God, and to remain with the father of lies, in misery, like unto himself." (2 Nephi 9:7, 9.) As Elder Boyd K. Packer testified, "I readily confess that I would find no peace, neither happiness nor safety, in a world without repentance. I do not know what I should do if there were no way for me to erase my mistakes. The agony would be more than I could bear."[4] "O how great the goodness of our God," declared Jacob, "who prepareth a way for our escape from the grasp of this awful monster; yea, that monster, death and hell" (2 Nephi 9:10). The way has been prepared that troubled souls can be soothed and calmed. The stains of sin can be cleansed. Hope can replace despair and the tears of sinful sorrow can be wiped off our faces. Joy can swallow up guilt. "Though your sins be as scarlet, they shall be as white as snow; though they be red like crimson, they shall be as wool" (Isaiah 1:18). We need not carry life's heaviest burden any longer. The terrible price for our iniquities has already been paid for us if we will heed the Savior's warning:

> And surely every man must repent or suffer. . . .
>
> Therefore I command you to repent—repent, lest I smite you by the rod of my mouth, and by my wrath, and by my anger, and your sufferings be sore—how sore you know not, how exquisite you know not, yea, how hard to bear you know not.
>
> For behold, I, God, have suffered these things for all, that they might not suffer if they would repent;
>
> But if they would not repent they must suffer even as I;
>
> Which suffering caused myself, even God, the greatest of all, to tremble because of pain, and to bleed at every pore, and to suffer both body and spirit—and would that I might not drink the bitter cup, and shrink—
>
> Nevertheless, glory be to the Father, and I partook and finished my preparations unto the children of men.
>
> Wherefore, I command you again to repent, lest I humble you with my almighty power. (D&C 19:4, 15–20.)

This incomprehensible suffering of the Savior was thus a vicarious suffering. It was *our* suffering—"inexpressible horrors"—which the Lord willingly and lovingly took upon himself in order that we might be spared such torment if we repent. Though he, of himself, was sinless and thus would not have had to experience in any degree the penalty for sin, he could not bear to let us suffer when he had the power to intercede in our behalf. Why would he willingly consent to such unfathomable and unspeakable suffering when we as mere mortals shrink from comparatively infinitesimal discomfiture? Why? Because of his infinite and incomprehensible love for us.

Notes

1. "Harbor of Forgiveness," *Church News*, 30 January 1988, p. 16; as quoted by Thomas S. Monson in "You Make a Difference," *Ensign*, May 1988, p. 42.

2. Richard L. Evans, *Richard Evans' Quote Book* (Salt Lake City: Publishers Press, 1971), p. 148.

3. Boyd K. Packer, *"That All May Be Edified"* (Salt Lake City: Bookcraft, 1982), pp. 63–64; italics added.

4. Boyd K. Packer, "Atonement, Agency, Accountability," *Ensign*, May 1988, p. 71.

2

Encircled in the Arms of God's Love

Often growing out of the many debilitating by-products of sin is a notion that may become a seemingly insurmountable obstacle to repentance. It is the idea that because of our sinfulness we are *unlovable* and *unforgivable*. This mistaken impression is often voiced in such common questions as "After what I have done, how can the Lord still love me? How can I ever be forgiven?" As we entangle ourselves in Satan's evil web, each of us is subject, to a greater or lesser degree, to these doubts. Elder Jeffrey R. Holland, then president of Brigham Young University, described those dangerous, sin-induced emotions to which Satan desires us to succumb:

> There are multitudes of men and women—in and out of the Church—who are struggling vainly against obstacles in their path. Many are fighting the battle of life —and losing. Indeed, there are those among us who consider themselves the vilest of sinners. . . .

How many broken hearts remain broken because those people feel they are beyond the pale of God's restorative power? How many bruised and battered spirits are certain that they have sunk to a depth at which the light of redeeming hope and grace will never again shine?[1]

Satan would have us feel that we cannot possibly be loved by our Heavenly Father or Jesus Christ after we have defiled ourselves with worldly ways. Satan delights in creating in us a belief that it is impossible for us to be completely forgiven and cleansed from the stains of sin. He knows that the feelings of being unlovable and unforgivable are towering roadblocks to repentance. These emotional obstacles become so difficult to surmount that too frequently some will give up in despair —thus sinking deeper into the quicksands of temptation. Elder Neal A. Maxwell cautioned:

Sometimes when we emphasize that, in a sense, he who has broken any divine law has broken all divine laws, in that he needs to "apply the atoning blood of Christ," we fail to perceive that the wrongdoer can become genuinely despondent about the prospects of ever being forgiven. While wallowing in deep despair, true repentance is impossible. The feeling of futility can render one powerless to further resist the adversary; it can blur the vital difference between understanding the possibility of forgiveness for the sinner, while rejecting the sinful act.[2]

How can we overcome these sometimes overwhelming ill-inspired feelings which seem to chain us down, especially when we feel unworthy to approach the only being who can deliver us? We will find relief only as we "lay hold upon the word of God, which is quick and powerful, which shall divide asunder all the cunning and the snares and the wiles of the devil, and lead the man of Christ in a strait and narrow course across that everlasting gulf of misery" (Helaman 3:29). It is in the scriptures that hope for the hopeless may be found. To those whose hearts are heavy with emotions of unworthiness and spiritual rejection, the scriptures resound with the motivating message of God's perfect and divine love for all mankind and the miracle of God's forgiveness that is available to all.

The Divine Love of God

Mortal men and women often reject friends or family members because they have committed serious sins or sometimes petty offenses. It is not at all unusual for a person to withhold love from someone who has betrayed a sacred trust or has been unfaithful to covenants or commitments. While this is often the response by human beings, it is certainly never the case with God. Jeremiah taught, "The Lord hath appeared of old unto me, saying, Yea, I have loved thee with an everlasting love: therefore with lovingkindness have I drawn thee" (Jeremiah 31:3). The scriptures clearly attest that although "the Lord cannot look upon sin with the least degree of allowance" (D&C 1:31), his love for us is a perfect, divine love. While others may reject us or withhold love because of our sins and unworthy ways, God stands ever ready to encircle us about with his "everlasting love." The Apostle Paul boldly declared that nothing, "neither death, nor life, nor angels, nor principalities, nor powers, nor things present, nor things to come, nor height, nor depth, nor any other creature, shall be able to separate us from the love of God" (see Romans 8:35–39). No matter who you are, no matter how low and unworthy you may feel, you are not rejected, nor alone, nor forgotten—God loves you still. "Certainly the Lord loves the sinner," wrote President Spencer W. Kimball, "and especially the one who is trying to repent, even though the sin is abhorrent to him. . . . The image of a loving, forgiving God comes through clearly to those who read and understand the scriptures. . . . He naturally desires to raise us up, not to push us down, to help us live, not to bring about our spiritual death."[3]

"I will love them freely," God told the prophet Hosea (Hosea 14:4). This perfect and divine love of God is indeed given freely to mankind. Two stories from the scriptures profoundly teach the unique nature of God's love for us. Each highlights a different aspect of his everlasting love, and each can help us overcome these roadblocks to repentance.

The Prodigal Son: The Perfect Love of a Father

Luke chapter 15 records three of the Savior's most familiar and significant parables—the parables of the lost sheep, the lost coin, and the prodigal son. Each of these parables symbolically depicts God's rejoicing over the repentance of the rebellious and wayward. As well as the main theme, a parable often contains more subtle messages that are also profoundly instructive. Such is the case with the Savior's parable of the prodigal son. A poignant message of unfailing paternal love comes through clearly in the following exchange between the prodigal and his father upon the return of that rebellious son to his home:

> And he arose, and came to his father. But when he was yet a great way off, his father saw him, and had compassion, and ran, and fell on his neck, and kissed him.
>
> And the son said unto him, Father, I have sinned against heaven, and in thy sight, and am no more worthy to be called thy son.
>
> But the Father said to his servants, Bring forth the best robe, and put it on him; and put a ring on his hand, and shoes on his feet:
>
> And bring hither the fatted calf, and kill it; and let us eat, and be merry:
>
> For this my son was dead, and is alive again; he was lost, and is found. (Luke 15:20–24.)

Here is not just a celebration for the returning profligate, but also a lesson in divine, perfect love. As readers of the parable we are left unaware of the extent of the repentance shown by the prodigal. While we are left to wonder, it is significant to note that the father does not pause to take a mental inventory of the prodigal's penitence or to question him regarding future resolve, but rather rushes to him in love and compassion. Reading between the lines of this parable, we can almost see that father, long before this emotional reunion, weeping for his wayward son, praying for his safety, hoping for his return, and through it all being unwavering in his fatherly love for his son. Undoubtedly he was pained by the actions of his wayward son. He could not condone the "riotous living," the blatant disregard for parental teachings so lovingly given. Despite the emotional wounds inflicted and the tears shed, his father still loved that son. Similarly our Father in Heaven continues to love us *even when we are wayward* because he is literally the Father of our spirits. Speaking of this parable and its significance, Elder Vaughn J. Featherstone said, "I think I have an understanding of what the Lord was trying to teach in this beautiful parable which extends hope to all. . . . [God's] love and compassion are eternally surrounding every soul who walks the earth."[4] We must never lose sight of the fact. God's great paternal love is *unconditional*, as explained by Elder Ronald E. Poelman:

> God is our Father; he loves us; his love is infinite and unconditional. His sorrow is great when we disobey his commandments and break his laws. He cannot condone our transgressions, but he loves us and wants us to return to him. I know of no greater inducement to repentance and reconciliation with him than an awareness of his love for us personally and individually.[5]

The Bride and the Bridegroom: The Perfect Love of a Savior

The symbolic story of the marriage of the ancient prophet Hosea to his wife Gomer is the second scriptural example that illustrates the nature of God's divine love for us as we struggle with the temptations and sins that beset us in this life. There is some question among scripture scholars concerning the historicity of this story. Because of the unusual nature of the Lord's commandment to the prophet Hosea to marry the harlot Gomer (Hosea chapters 1–2), some feel that this is not an actual event but rather an allegory used to teach an important principle.[6] Whether the marriage was actual or allegorical is irrelevant to the message of divine love and forgiveness found therein.

Most often this story is used to teach the concept of the gathering of Israel. There is no doubt that the symbolism of this story has direct application to the destruction and dispersion of ancient Israel. It clearly shows the mercy and love of God in extending his hand to gather Israel. In addition to this collective interpretation there is also a relevant message for individual lives as well.

Although Gomer was a harlot, representative of wayward Israel or each of us, Hosea, representing Jehovah, had forgiven her of her sinful past and loved her immensely. She had given him three children. Our hearts break for Hosea as we read that Gomer then rejected him as her husband, abandoned her family, and returned to a life of harlotry. Many of us might feel that if we were in Hosea's situation we would be justified in casting her off forever. We would feel betrayed and deeply hurt, as Hosea must also have felt. But as we examine this story more closely, we cannot help but marvel at the continued compassion and love that Hosea demonstrated for his wicked wife. Of course, he abhorred her adulterous actions. He could not minimize the severity of her sins or ignore her infidelity; but he loved her still and his heart yearned for her return. The Prophet Isaiah interpreted the spiritual symbolism of the husband and the wayward bride, of which Hosea and Gomer are examples:

> For thy Maker is thine husband; the Lord of Hosts is his name; and thy Redeemer the Holy One of Israel; The God of the whole earth shall he be called.
>
> For the Lord hath called thee as a woman forsaken and grieved in spirit, and a wife of youth, when thou wast refused, saith thy God.
>
> For a small moment have I forsaken thee, but with great mercies will I gather thee. (Isaiah 54:5–7.)

Thus the Savior is sometimes characterized in the scriptures as the bridegroom and we, collectively and individually, are his bride. Just as Gomer was unfaithful to Hosea and to the covenants she had made with him, each of us to some degree has also been remiss. We all have neglected our spiritual duties and some have even broken covenants. Despite our unfaithfulness and slothfulness we are loved with "the love of Christ, which passeth knowledge" (Ephesians 3:19). The depth of his love for us is unfathomable because he "bought [us] with a price" (1 Corinthians 6:20). "His atoning and redemptive suffering in Gethsemane and on Golgotha's hill," declared Elder Vaughn J. Featherstone, "are the greatest acts of love ever performed."[7] Though some of the blessings of the atonement of Christ are *conditioned* upon our righteousness, the Savior's love is extended to all *unconditionally*. This godly love is illustrated by his response to the woman caught in adultery (see John 8:1–11). While the angry mob stood by anxious to administer justice by stoning according to the ancient law, Jesus quietly declared, "He that is without sin among you, let him first cast a stone at her" (John 8:7). Commenting on this episode and the symbolism of the Savior's response, Elder Marvin J. Ashton said:

> He stooped down and wrote on the ground. They heard what he said. . . . Convicted by their own conscience they left on their own, not driven away. They went out one by one—not to find stones, but to nurse their spiritual wounds. . . . Left alone with the woman, he said, "Where are those thine accusers? hath no man condemned thee?" . . .
>
> The woman taken in adultery answered the Lord's question regarding her accusers by saying, "No man, Lord." And then this powerful declaration came: "Go, and sin no more." The Master was teaching in that day and also teaching in this very hour. His great message: Despise the sin, but love the sinner. I hope that can give us strength and confidence and a closer relationship to our Savior Jesus Christ. Jesus did not condone adultery. He gave the woman love instead of an authoritative lecture. She and the accusers needed a lesson in love. The situation called for mercy and compassion.

How rewarding it is to know that Jesus believed that man is greater than all of his sins. Is it any wonder he was referred to as the "Good Shepherd"? He loved all of his sheep whether they were strays, hungry, helpless, cold, or lost.[8]

Nephi also recognized the Savior's divine love for us in his movingly prophetic description of the Messiah's mortal ministry:

> And the world, because of their iniquity, shall judge him to be a thing of naught; wherefore they scourge him, and he suffereth it; and they smite him, and he suffereth it. Yea, they spit upon him, and he suffereth it, because of his loving kindness and his long-suffering towards the children of men. (1 Nephi 19:9.)

Later Nephi observed, "He doeth not anything save it be for the benefit of the world; for he loveth the world, even that he layeth down his own life that he may draw all men unto him" (2 Nephi 26:24).

We will receive, even in wickedness, the Savior's love and compassion. This perfect love for us, evident even in the premortal realm when he willingly accepted his foreordained redemptive role, was excruciatingly enhanced in Gethsemane and on Golgotha. "He suffereth the pains of all men," Jacob testified, "yea, the pains of every living creature, both men, women, and children, who belong to the family of Adam" (2 Nephi 9:21). Our love for our Redeemer increases as we recognize the infinite price he was willing to pay for us and thus begin to sense his divine love. "We love him," wrote John the Beloved, "because he first loved us" (1 John 4:19). Elder Rex D. Pinegar declared:

> All of us should remember that while we are commanded to love God, he has a *perfect* love for us. All the world needs to be taught of the great redeeming power of the Savior's love. He loves us so much that he has promised to forgive us of those things we do that are wrong and remember them no more if we will only repent and come unto him. . . .

He loves us so much that he was willing to pay the price for those sins. He suffered for us. He died for us. He said, Come follow me; cast your burdens on the Lord. His desire is to lift us, to help us, to guide us, to save us.[9]

Some are motivated to begin the process of repentance out of guilt or fear; some by a sense of embarrassment or shame; some are motivated by being "caught" and therefore compelled to change by the dramatic consequences of their sins. Any of these motivations may induce the *action* of repentance, but the most powerful catalyst for an enduring *attitude* of repentance is love—the perfect, divine, and unconditional love of God, our Father, and Jesus Christ, our Savior. "Repenting" out of fear, humiliation, or embarrassment will seldom bring about a long-lasting transformation. A genuine repentance process begins only as we realize this matchless eternal love for us and exercise a renewed faith in Christ. Sensing and accepting in faith that sacred love can help us to overcome our feelings of being unlovable and to set our sights on the spiritual transformation that comes only through the atonement of Jesus Christ. "If we could feel or were sensitive even in the slightest," declared Elder David B. Haight, "to the matchless love of our Savior and his willingness to suffer for our individual sins, we would cease procrastination and 'clean the slate,' and repent of all our transgressions."[10]

Lehi and Nephi testified of this sustaining and motivating influence of God's love. "I am encircled about eternally," testified Lehi, "in the arms of his love" (2 Nephi 1:15). Even the great Nephi, with all his prophetic powers and spiritual strengths, had moments when he wrestled with his own unworthiness and fallibility. Yet he rejoiced in the mercy of the Lord and acknowledged the actuating power of God's perfect love:

Notwithstanding the great goodness of the Lord, in showing me his great and marvelous works, my heart exclaimeth: O wretched man that I am! Yea, my heart sorroweth because of my flesh; my soul grieveth because of mine iniquities.

I am encompassed about, because of the temptations and the sins which do so easily beset me.

And when I desire to rejoice, my heart groaneth because of my sins; nevertheless, I know in whom I have trusted.

My God hath been my support; he hath led me through mine afflictions. . . .

He hath filled me with his love, even unto the consuming of my flesh. . . .

Awake, my soul! No longer droop in sin. Rejoice, O my heart, and give place no more for the enemy of my soul. . . .

Rejoice, O my heart, and cry unto the Lord, and say: O Lord, I will praise thee forever; yea, my soul will rejoice in thee, my God, and the rock of my salvation. (2 Nephi 4:17–21, 28, 30.)

Like Nephi, when we begin to sense that divine love we too will desire to "no longer droop in sin." We could not be so profoundly motivated to repent without a knowledge that our Heavenly Father's love is perfect and unconditional. Likewise the Savior's infinite love is designed to draw all men unto him that they might yearn to partake of the mercy and forgiveness that he lovingly and willingly extends to all who come unto him through repentance.

The Availability of the Miracle of Forgiveness

While we can conquer sin-induced feelings of being *unlovable* through faith in the scriptural teachings of the nature of God's love, we may also struggle with another sentiment that often accompanies transgression. It is the feeling that through our wickedness we are *unforgivable*. With the exceptions of murder and the sin against the Holy Ghost, this idea is also mistaken. President Harold B. Lee described Satan's desire that we experience this despair and despondency: "Satan would have you think . . . and [would] some-times persuade you that now having made one mistake, you might go on and on with no turning back. That is one of the great falsehoods. *The miracle of forgiveness is available to all of those who turn from their evil doings and return no more. . . .* Have that in mind, all of you who may be troubled with a burden of sin."[11]

As President Lee explained, the miracle of mercy and forgiveness is available; but unlike the divine love of God, it is available only upon a *conditional* basis. His approbation of our lives, his forgiveness of our sins, and his acceptance of us into his presence is conditional upon the terms of the infinite and eternal Atonement, terms that were established "according to the great plan of the Eternal God" (see Alma 34:8–10) before the foundation of the world. The Father's love for us is *unconditional* by virtue of his eternal patriarchal relationship to us, but his blessings (of which forgiveness of sins is only one) are *conditional* upon obedience to laws. "There is a law, irrevocably decreed in heaven before the foundations of this world, upon which all blessings are predicated—and when we obtain any blessing from God, it is by obedience to that law upon which it is predicated" (D&C 130:20–21).

The scriptural story of Hosea's marriage to Gomer and the parable of the prodigal son also point out this principle. In Hosea chapter 3 we see that although Hosea's love for his wayward wife was continual and unconditional, his forgiveness and reacceptance of her as his wife was based on conditions of penitence—a desire to return to her family, a willingness to abandon her wicked ways and abominable associations, and a commitment to renewed devotion and faithfulness.

In a similar vein, we can see in the parable of the prodigal son the distinction between the father's unconditional love for his son and his bestowal of birthright blessings. The elder son, who had been true to his birthright, was troubled by his father's reaction to the return of his profligate brother. He misunderstood the ring, the robe, and the rejoicing and feasting—evidences of the father's unconditional love—to be signs of total forgiveness.

Now his elder son was in the field: and as he came and drew nigh to the house, he heard musick and dancing.

And he called one of the servants, and asked what these things meant.

And he said unto him, Thy brother is come; and thy father hath killed the fatted calf, because he hath received him safe and sound,

And he was angry, and would not go in: therefore came his father out, and intreated him.

And he answering said to his father, Lo, these many years do I serve thee, neither transgressed I at any time thy commandment: and yet thou never gavest me a kid, that I might make merry with my friends:

But as soon as this thy son was come, which hath devoured thy living with harlots, thou hast killed for him the fatted calf.

And he said unto him, *Son, thou art ever with me, and all that I have is thine.*

It was meet that we should make merry, and be glad: for this thy brother was dead, and is alive again; and was lost, and is found. (Luke 15:25–32; italics added.)

Implicit in the father's response to the concerns of the faithful son is the lesson that compassion and love, however powerful and profound, are not guarantors of forgiveness. We must become worthy to receive that miracle and blessing in our lives. The Savior, as our "spiritual husband," stands willing to forgive us of our evils and unfaithfulness. "I stand at the door, and knock," the Savior declared, [and] "if any man hear my voice, and open the door, I will come in to him, and will sup with him, and he with me" (Revelation 3:20). Note that we are the ones who must "hear" his voice and "open" the door. The scriptures are replete with invitations for us to partake of the mercy and forgiveness of Christ, but each reference resounds with an unmistakable message—*we* must return unto him and meet the conditions of repentance. The prophet Isaiah declared: "Let the wicked forsake his way, and the unrighteous man his thoughts: and let him return unto the Lord, and he will have mercy upon him; and to our God, for he will abundantly pardon" (Isaiah 55:7).

These invitations are extended to *all* who feel unforgivable—who view their lives and situations as hopelessly past the point of no return. Keeping in mind the two weighty exceptions designated by the Lord—murder and the sin against the Holy Ghost—there is no sin or sinner beyond the reach of Christ's infinite atonement. The Lord has emphatically declared to ancient and modern prophets that *all* who desire to be clean, to have the heavy burdens of sin lifted, to once again feel of God's divine approbation may receive the miracle of mercy *if* they will come to him, the Physician of men's souls, and be healed spiritually. "Come unto Christ, who is the Holy One of Israel," wrote Amaleki as he closed the book of Omni, "and partake of his salvation, and the power of his redemption. Yea, come unto him, and offer your whole souls as an offering unto him, and continue in fasting and praying, and endure to the end; and as the Lord liveth ye will be saved." (Omni 1:26.) Alma often reiterated the Lord's injunction to repent and partake of the miracle of forgiveness:

> Wo unto all ye workers of iniquity; repent, repent, for the Lord God hath spoken it!
>
> Behold, he sendeth an invitation unto all men, for the arms of mercy are extended towards them, and he saith: Repent, and I will receive you.
>
> Yea, he saith: Come unto me and ye shall partake of the fruit of the tree of life; yea, ye shall eat and drink of the bread and the waters of life freely;
>
> Yea, come unto me and bring forth works of righteousness. (Alma 5:32–34.)

> But God did call on men, in the name of his Son, (this being the plan of redemption which was laid) saying: If ye will repent, and harden not your hearts, then will I have mercy upon you, through mine Only Begotten Son;

Therefore, whosoever repenteth, and hardeneth not his heart, he shall have claim on mercy through mine Only Begotten Son, unto a remission of his sins; and these shall enter into my rest. (Alma 12:33–34.)

As the burden of sin becomes increasingly unbearable, Lucifer adds weight to the already heavy load by speaking lies to our wounded and weakened souls. "God can't love you after what you have done." "You cannot change." "You might as well give in to my enticements." "You have gone too far." "You can never be clean again!" These are but a few of his insidious heresies designed to rob us of all hope and direction. We must not fall prey to Lucifer's lies. The message of hope found in the scriptures brings comfort and a catalyst for change. You are loved! You can be forgiven! President Spencer W. Kimball has testified of this miracle:

God will wipe away from their eyes the tears of anguish, and remorse, and consternation, and fear, and guilt. Dry eyes will replace the wet ones, and smiles of satisfaction will replace the worried, anxious look.

What relief! What comfort! What joy! Those laden with transgressions and sorrows and sin may be forgiven and cleansed and purified if they will return to their Lord, learn of him, and keep his commandments. And all of us needing to repent of day-to-day follies and weaknesses can likewise share in this miracle.[12]

Even amidst the anguish of sin, we can reach for the divine love of our Father and our Savior that encircles us eternally. As we allow ourselves to be enveloped in the reality of their unconditional love, our hope for healing will be heightened and our ears will be more acutely attuned to the Master's invitation to partake of his mercy. Elder Richard G. Scott testified of God's love and counseled us to pray for the spiritual strength required for our repentance:

I cannot comprehend [God's] power, his majesty, his perfections. But I do understand something of his love, his compassion, his mercy.

There is no burden he cannot lift.

There is no heart he cannot purify and fill with joy.

There is no life he cannot cleanse and restore when one is obedient to his teachings. . . .

He is your Father; pray to him. If your life is in disarray and you feel uncomfortable and unworthy to pray because you are not clean, don't worry. He already knows about all of that. He is waiting for you to kneel in humility and take the first few steps. Pray for strength. Pray for others to be led to support you and guide you and lift you. Pray that the love of the Savior will pour into your heart. Pray that the miracle of the Atonement will bring forgiveness because you are willing to change. I know that those prayers will be answered, for God loves you. His Son gave his life for you. I know they will help you.[13]

When we feel *unlovable* and *unforgivable*, the Lord lovingly will teach us anew that we are not forsaken nor forgotten. "But, behold, Zion [and some of us individually] hath said: The Lord hath forsaken me, and my Lord hath forgotten me — but he will show that he hath not. For can a woman forget her sucking child, that she should not have compassion on the son of her womb? Yea, they may forget, yet will I not forget thee. . . . Behold, I have graven thee upon the palms of my hands; thy walls are continually before me." (See also 1 Nephi 21:14–16; Isaiah 49:14–16.)

Notes

1. Jeffrey R. Holland, *However Long and Hard the Road* (Salt Lake City: Deseret Book Co., 1985), p. 77.

2. Neal A. Maxwell, "Hope for the Hopeless," *The Instructor*, August 1966, p. 318.

3. Spencer W. Kimball, *The Miracle of Forgiveness* (Salt Lake City: Bookcraft, 1969), pp. 343–44.

4. Vaughn J. Featherstone, "However Faint the Light May Glow," *Ensign*, November 1982, p. 72.

5. Ronald E. Poelman, "God's Love for Us Transcends Our Transgressions," in *Love* (Salt Lake City: Deseret Book Co., 1986), p. 92.

6. See Sidney B. Sperry, *The Spirit of the Old Testament*, 2d ed. (Salt Lake City: Deseret Book Co., 1970), pp. 144–45.

7. Vaughn J. Featherstone, "However Faint the Light May Glow," *Ensign*, November 1982, p. 72.

8. Marvin J. Ashton, "Lessons from the Master," address delivered at seventeen-stake fireside, Brigham Young University, 5 June 1988.

9. Rex D. Pinegar, "The Gift of Love," in *Love*, p. 75.

10. David B. Haight, "Our Lord and Savior," *Ensign*, May 1988, p. 23.

11. Harold B. Lee, *Stand Ye in Holy Places* (Salt Lake City: Deseret Book Co., 1974), p. 185; italics added.

12. Spencer W. Kimball, *The Miracle of Forgiveness,* p. 368.

13. Richard G. Scott, "True Friends That Lift," *Ensign*, November 1988, p. 77.

3

"Faith unto Repentance"

Understanding God's infinite and perfect love for his children creates in us a desire to please him, to feel of his approbation, and to return to his merciful and compassionate arms. It is faith in the redemptive power of Christ, however, that transforms *desire* into *action*, and it is only by faith in the Lord Jesus Christ that enduring, profound repentance is possible. President Ezra Taft Benson has declared: "True repentance is based on and flows from faith in the Lord Jesus Christ. There is no other way."[1] Love of God and his Son may be the stimulus, but faith in the blood of the Lamb of God is the key to attaining true repentance.

In *Lectures on Faith* the Prophet Joseph Smith declared that "faith being the first principle in revealed religion, [is] the foundation of all righteousness."[2] Since repentance is a fundamental principle associated with righteousness, the Prophet's statement could also be paraphrased to read: "Faith is the foundation of all repentance." Faith in the Lord Jesus Christ as the first principle of the gospel is the foundation upon which repentance as the second principle must be built in order to be of any efficacy. (Compare Articles of Faith 1:4.) "Thus repentance follows faith," wrote Elder Bruce R. McConkie. "It is born of faith; it is the child of faith; and it operates only in the lives of those who have faith—faith in the Lord Jesus Christ. Faith comes first and repentance second; one is the first principle of the gospel, the other the second."[3] Elder Orson Pratt also held that true repentance is inseparably linked with faith in Christ.

> The first effect of true faith is a sincere, true, and thorough repentance of all sins. . . . No man has a saving faith without attending to [this requirement of repentance]. No person can be a believer in Christ, in the scriptural sense of that term, without complying in the strictest manner with these commandments. . . .
>
> A faith, then, that brings remission of sins or justification to the sinner, is that which is connected with repentance and baptism. . . . Faith is the starting point—the foundation and cause of our repentance.[4]

Since "a saving faith" is the crucial "starting point" of repentance, it will, as Elder Pratt continued, "in all cases lead to repentance," and will be the "moving cause of [repentance] which brings salvation."[5] Furthermore, actions or efforts to repent that are not firmly grounded in this faith in Christ will not produce a true repentance that results in forgiveness. Without fully comprehending that repentance is a fruit of faith, a person may go through a "repentance checklist" and sadly discover that the spiritual gift of peace of conscience that accompanies a remission of sins has eluded him. Or worse yet, he may feel fully satisfied that he has met all the "requirements" for repentance and not realize that his efforts have not been fully effective. "Checklist repentance" lacking the firm foundation of faith in the Redeemer may produce results similar to what the Prophet Isaiah described: "It shall even be as when an hungry man dreameth, and, behold, he eateth; but he awaketh, and his soul is empty: or as when a thirsty man dreameth, and, behold, he drinketh; but he awaketh, and, behold, he is faint, and his soul hath appetite" (Isaiah 29:8).

"Checklist Repentance" Versus True Repentance

Sometimes we teach repentance as a series of steps to be taken or items on a checklist to be completed for each sin that we may commit. Accompanying such teaching may be catchy phrases or words such as the "Rs of repentance." These are used to make it easier to teach and remember the various components of repentance. Such a checklist approach may serve well as a memory device or teaching method, but it does not accurately and completely teach the true doctrine of repentance. It may leave out "the weightier matters of the law." A well-intended emphasis on an enumerated list of *actions* of repentance may actually unwittingly deemphasize the absolute necessity of *attitudes* of repentance such as faith and "real intent." A preoccupation with outward performances may overshadow the inward "workings of the Spirit" that will ultimately result in a thorough transformation of life. "The eternal significance of action or inaction," wrote Elder Dallin H. Oaks, "turns on the state of mind that motivated the act or omission. Acts that seem to be good bring blessings only when they are done with a good motive, with real and righteous intent."[6] Such is certainly the case with repentance. The familiar "Rs" or other similar approaches to repentance are good and important actions, but they will not produce a remission of sins without the good motive, the real and righteous intent that springs from true faith in Christ. The dangers and deficiencies of a "checklist" aproach to repentance can be seen in the following true stories.

A young lady approached the bishop of her ward minutes before sacrament meeting. "I need to talk with you," she told the bishop. The bishop looked at his watch and attempted to make an appointment with her after the meeting. She insisted that it would only take a moment.

"Last night I committed fornication," she announced to the bishop. "I am here to confess that transgression to you since I know that confession is one of the steps of repentance."

The bishop explained that they would need to meet together right after sacrament meeting to discuss the matter further, resolve problems, and talk about the true meaning of repentance. She resisted and responded that she could not understand why an additional interview would be necessary since she had already *recognized* her sin, felt *remorse, confessed* to the bishop, and *resolved* that the sinful act would not happen again. In her mind she had completed all of the "steps of repentance" that she had been taught. Yet she demonstrated little understanding of or appreciation for the fundamental role of faith in Christ and his atonement in the repentance process. She seemed to be lacking the inward *attitudes* that more accurately reflect true penitence.

A young man was appearing before a Church court. He had confessed a major moral transgression to the proper priesthood authority. At the conclusion of the proceedings the presiding authority asked him to talk about his feelings. "Tell us how you feel about repentance," the stake president asked. "Share with us your innermost feelings."

The young man bristled at the request. "What do my feelings have to do with it anyway?" he retorted with disgust. "I have done everything required of me to repent. I have completed all of the steps of the repentance process. What more is there for me to do? I have made a complete *confession*, made the proper *restitution*, and have resolved the matter. Isn't that repentance? My feelings are personal and are none of your business. They are irrelevant, since I have *done* all of the steps of repentance." This young man had focused his efforts on a series of designated *actions* but had rejected the notion that true repentance must also encompass *attitudes* which give life and power to the outward observance.

These true-to-life case studies are representative of hundreds of examples of people, young and old, most with good intentions and noble motives, who view repentance merely as a series of steps to be taken or actions to be completed rather than an all-encompassing process of being, changing, feeling, *and* doing. The remarks of Elder Theodore M. Burton of the First Quroum of the Seventy seem to confirm that this is a fairly common misconception in the Church:

> Just what *is* repentance? Actually it is easier for me to tell you what repentance is *not* than to tell you what repentance *is*.
>
> My present assignment as a General Authority is to assist the First Presidency. I prepare information for them to use in considering applications to readmit transgressors into the Church and to restore priesthood and/or temple blessings. Many times a bishop will write: "I feel he has suffered enough!" But suffering is not repentance. Suffering comes from *lack* of complete repentance. A stake president will write: "I feel he has been punished enough!" But punishment is not repentance. Punishment *follows* disobedience and *precedes* repentance. A husband will write: "My wife has confessed everything!" But confession is not repentance. Confession is an admission of guilt that occurs *as* repentance begins. A wife will write: "My husband is filled with remorse!" But remorse is not repentance. Remorse and sorrow continue because a person has *not* yet fully repented.[7]

A "checklist" approach to repentance might also be called "recipe repentance." A bread recipe contains a listing of all of the ingredients, but merely placing the ingredients in a mixing bowl does not constitute making bread. A successful bread baker knows that in addition to using high quality ingredients, he or she must carefully mix them, knead and work the dough, and then allow the yeast to cause the dough to rise adequately. Without this careful attention to the nurturing and working of the dough, the bread will be less than desirable regardless of the quality of the ingredients. Similarly, the "Rs of repentance" or any other combination of "ingredients" must be coupled with careful nurturing and leavening that is obtainable only through faith in the Lord Jesus Christ. Elder James E. Talmage described how the "ingredients" of repentance are dependent upon the leavening of faith.

The term repentance . . . as representing the duty required of all who would obtain forgiveness for transgression . . . indicates a godly sorrow for sin, producing a reformation of life, and embodies (1) a conviction of guilt; (2) a desire to be relieved from the hurtful effects of sin; and (3) an earnest determination to forsake sin and to accomplish good. Repentance is a result of contrition of soul, which springs from a deep sense of humility, and this in turn is dependent upon the exercise of an abiding faith in God.[8]

The Deficiencies of "Checklist Repentance"

When we view repentance as a mere checklist of items that must be completed for *every* sin committed, we fall prey to the spiritual dangers and doctrinal deficiencies of such a superficial approach. Three main deficiencies, with their potential pitfalls, are evident.

First, under such a program a person may never really get "caught up." As one goes through the "requirements" of repentance, he will find that he has committed other sins that also need his attention. To apply the "checklist" to every sin ever committed would be like taking one step forward and two steps back. It would be impossible to conscientiously go through the process for every sin. This creates the very real dilemma of discouragement for someone who is trying to repent from a "recipe card." Reflecting this quandary, questions often arise such as "How can I repent for things I did years ago? How can I *recognize, confess,* or *make restitution* for sins I can no longer remember?" In such a situation it would be easy for one to become so discouraged about repentance that he may actually give up in despair and slip deeper into the quicksands of sin.

A second deficiency of "recipe card repentance' is that for some sins and situations there are not enough "Rs of repentance." For other sins there are items on the "checklist" of repentance that cannot be completely fulfilled. President Spencer W. Kimball wrote that "there are some sins for which no adequate restitution can be made, and others for which only partial restitution is possible."[9] The underlying premise and logic of "checklist repentance" would make repentance appear futile under such circumstances. Bruce C. Hafen, former president of Ricks College, warned about the pitfalls of this mistaken thinking when he taught:

> Many, for whom the repentance process asks more than they can give, take for granted that they are fully responsible to compensate for their own sins; then they discover hopelessly that they lack the power to make full compensation by themselves. . . . There aren't enough "Rs" in the steps of repentance, not enough power of restoration within the limits of human ability. . . . Until those in such predicaments find the Savior at the heart of the Atonement . . . there is no complete escape and final relief. Because we lack the power to compensate fully for the effects of our transgression, we are utterly dependent upon Christ, no matter how earnest our repentance.[10]

President Hafen's thoughtful statement also exposes the third and most important deficiency of "checklist repentance." When we overemphasize "steps" or outward actions we tend to elevate man's doings at the expense of Christ's cleansing power. We make repentance appear as though it is something that we can *do* by ourselves. Such a serious misconception minimizes the miraculous atonement of Jesus Christ and the grace of God that grants us forgiveness. When we focus all of our attention and efforts on the things *we* must do to repent, we tend to overlook what *he* did to make repentance possible. "Repentance is one of the gifts of God to fallen man," wrote Elder Orson Pratt. "The great and infinite sacrifice, made by the Son of God, for the sins of the world, has purchased for man the gift of Repentance, which, if properly received and exercised, will give him claim upon the mercy of God against whom he has sinned."[11] Moroni taught that perfection and remission of sins do not come merely from our own actions, however important these acts are. They only have efficacy "through the shedding of the blood of Christ."

> Yea, come unto Christ, and be perfected in him, and deny yourselves of all ungodliness; and if ye shall deny yourselves of all ungodliness, and love God with all your might, mind and strength, then is his grace sufficient for you, that by his grace ye may be perfect in Christ; and if by the grace of God ye are perfect in Christ, ye can in nowise deny the power of God.
>
> And again, if ye by the grace of God are perfect in Christ, and deny not his power, then are ye sanctified in Christ by the grace of God, through the shedding of the blood of Christ, which is in the covenant of the Father unto the remission of your sins, that ye become holy, without spot. (Moroni 10:32–33.)

An emphasis on "checklist" or "recipe" repentance personifies "psuedo-self-reliance." As Robert L. Millet has insightfully stated, "We must never allow the need for self-reliance to rob us of the power of Christ which we might enjoy."[12] Thus the worst danger of this narrow view of repentance is that it all too often causes us to leave out the most important element, the most important "R of repentance"—*Redeemer*.

Relying upon Him Who Is Mighty to Save

The scriptures—especially the Book of Mormon—are replete with examples and teachings on faith as the enabling ingredient in repentance. The prophet Enos left us his account of what he characterized as "the wrestle which I had before God, before I received a remission of my sins." He learned firsthand from the Lord the central role of faith in true repentance.

> I went to hunt beasts in the forests; and the words which I had often heard my father speak concerning eternal life, and the joy of the saints, sunk deep into my heart.
>
> And my soul hungered; and I kneeled down before my Maker, and I cried unto him in mighty prayer and supplication for mine own soul; and all the day long

did I cry unto him; yea, and when the night came I did still raise my voice high that it reached the heavens.

And there came a voice unto me, saying: Enos, thy sins are forgiven thee, and thou shalt be blessed.

And I, Enos, knew that God could not lie; wherefore, my guilt was swept away.

And I said: Lord, how is it done?

And he said unto me: Because of thy faith in Christ . . . thy faith hath made thee whole. (Enos 1:3–8.)

The Lord simply stated that it was faith in Christ that finally brought about the remission of Enos's sins, and not so much the various outward actions of repentance, as important as they are. Nephi teaches that we cannot save ourselves merely through our own deeds but must have "unshaken faith in [Christ], relying wholly upon the merits of him who is mighty to save" (2 Nephi 31:19). The actual remission of sins comes to us as a gift of God through this faith. When we are willing to rely "wholly upon the merits of him who is mighty to save" we will then submit to the designated requirements of repentance as a natural outgrowth of faith rather than from a rote or ritualistic adherence to a checklist. Our actions and attitudes of penitence become evidence of our faith and not a substitute for it. While we may indeed be judged by our *works*, we are nonetheless justified by our *faith*.

The prophet Amulek, in the Book of Mormon, also taught that it is "the great and last sacrifice" of Jesus Christ that gives power and efficacy to the doctrine of repentance. He emphatically declared that *faith must precede repentance* in order for the mercy of the Messiah to be enjoyed.

And behold, this is the whole meaning of the law, every whit pointing to that great and last sacrifice; and that great and last sacrifice will be the Son of God, yea, infinite and eternal.

And thus he shall bring salvation to all those who shall *believe on his name*; this being the intent of this last sacrifice, to bring about the bowels of mercy, which overpowereth justice, and bringeth about means unto men that they may have *faith unto repentance*.

And thus mercy can satisfy the demands of justice, and encircles them in the arms of safety, while he that exercises no *faith unto repentance* is exposed to the whole law of the demands of justice; therefore *only unto him that has faith unto repentance is brought about the great and eternal plan of redemption.*

Therefore may God grant unto you, my brethren, that ye may *begin to exercise your faith unto repentance*, that ye begin to call upon his holy name, that he would have mercy upon you;

Yea, cry unto him for mercy; for he is mighty to save. (Alma 34:14–18; italics added.)

Perhaps no scriptural example better illustrates Amulek's teaching of "faith unto repentance" and the need to "cry unto [Christ] for mercy" than the story of the dramatic conversion of Alma the Younger. Alma's heartrending account reveals a sinner who is "racked with torment" and "harrowed up by the memory of [his] many sins," who pleads with the Savior to do for him something that he cannot do for himself. Again, we do not see Alma mechanically going through a series of steps to repentance. In fact, there is no recorded evidence that he had previously performed any of those actions traditionally taught as sequential steps to forgiveness. We see, however, that the miracle of forgiveness in Alma's sudden change from a life of sin to a life of service resulted from "faith unto repentance."

And it came to pass that as I was thus racked with torment, while I was harrowed up by the memory of my many sins, behold, I remembered also to have heard my father prophesy unto the people concerning the coming of one Jesus Christ, a Son of God, to atone for the sins of the world.

Now, as my mind caught hold upon this thought, I cried within my heart: O Jesus, thou Son of God, have mercy on me, who am in the gall of bitterness, and am encircled about by the everlasting chains of death.

And now, behold, when I thought this, I could remember my pains no more; yea, I was harrowed up by the memory of my sins no more.

And oh, what joy, and what marvelous light I did behold; yea, my soul was filled with joy as exceeding as was my pain! (Alma 36:17–20.)

The merciful relief was extended to Alma because of his newly exercised faith in the atonement of Christ. The abandonment of his sinful practices, the restitution for past mistakes, and a life of continued commitment to the kingdom of God grew out of this faith in Christ. Another scriptural example also affirms this principle. Nephi saw in vision, nearly six hundred years earlier, the Savior's twelve Apostles. "And, behold, they are righteous forever; for because of their faith in the Lamb of God their garments are made white in his blood," declared an angel to Nephi. "These are made white in the blood of the Lamb, because of their faith in him." (1 Nephi 12:8–11.) The cleansing of our garments comes to us, as it did to Enos, Alma, and the ancient apostles, not because of our own righteous acts but "because of the righteousness of thy Redeemer" (2 Nephi 2:3)—because of his infinite atonement.

Indeed, faith in Christ as the first principle and repentance as the second principle, along with all other principles and ordinances of the gospel, are totally dependent upon the atoning sacrifice of our Lord Jesus Christ. "Nothing in the entire plan of salvation compares in any way in importance with . . . the atoning sacrifice of our Lord. . . . It is the rock foundation upon which the gospel and all other things rest," wrote Elder Bruce R. McConkie. "The doctrine of the *Atonement* embraces, sustains, supports, and gives life and force to all other gospel doctrines. It is the foundation upon which all truth rests, and all things grow out of it and come because of it."[13]

Comparing the principles and ordinances of the gospel to a wheel can illustrate the relationship of repentance and other requirements for salvation to the atonement of Christ. In this

analogy, the *hub* must be the Atonement, and all other principles including repentance are merely *spokes*. For this
"gospel wheel" to function properly the spokes must be
securely attached to the hub. Through this example it is easy
to see that actions and attitudes of repentance not founded
upon or growing out of sincere faith would be like individual,
unattached spokes of a wheel. Spokes alone have no value to
a wheel without the center hub as anchor. Elder Bruce R. Mc-
Conkie declared:

> Suppose we have the scriptures, the gospel, the priest-
> hood, the Church, the ordinances, the organization,
> even the keys of the kingdom—everything that now is
> down to the last jot and tittle—and yet there is no
> atonement of Christ. What then? Can we be saved? Will
> all our good works save us? Will we be rewarded for all
> our righteousness?
>
> Most assuredly we will not. We are not saved by
> works alone, no matter how good; we are saved be-
> cause God sent his Son to shed his blood in Geth-
> semane and on Calvary that all through him might ran-
> somed be. We are saved by the blood of Christ.
>
> To paraphrase Abinadi: "Salvation doth not come
> by the Church alone: and were it not for the Atone-
> ment, given by the grace of God as a free gift, all men
> must unavoidably perish, and this notwithstanding the
> Church and all that appertains to it."[14]

Truly, then, repentance stems only from faith in the redemptive and cleansing power of the blood of the Lamb of
God. Without the merciful Atonement there could be no forgiveness of our sins. Thus, as Nephi taught, "it is by grace that
we are saved, after all we can do" (2 Nephi 25:23). While
there really is no set "recipe" or checklist of steps that must
be taken in every case of repentance, we must still do "all we
can do." The Lord himself has specified that "all we can do"
begins with an "unshaken faith" in Christ. Other than this, he
has given us no list of "Rs"—only a simple but profound formula which encompasses all other attitudes and actions of re-

pentance. He declared (see D&C 58:42–43): "By this ye may know if a man repenteth of his sins—behold, he will confess them and forsake them."

Notes

1. Ezra Taft Benson, *The Teachings of Ezra Taft Benson* (Salt Lake City: Bookcraft, 1988), p. 71.

2. Joseph Smith, *Lectures on Faith,* compiled by N. B. Lundwall (Salt Lake City: N. B. Lundwall, Publisher, 1940), p. 7.

3. Bruce R. McConkie, *A New Witness for the Articles of Faith* (Salt Lake City: Deseret Book Co., 1985), p. 217.

4. Orson Pratt, "True Faith," *A Series of Pamphlets by Orson Pratt* (Liverpool: Franklin D. Richards, 1852), pp. 5–6; as quoted in *A Compilation Containing the Lectures on Faith,* compiled by N. B. Lundwall (Salt Lake City: N. B. Lundwall, Publisher, 1940), pp. 76–77.

5. Ibid., p. 6. (See also Lundwall, p. 77.)

6. Dallin H. Oaks, *Pure in Heart* (Salt Lake City: Bookcraft, 1988), pp. 147–48.

7. Theodore M. Burton, "The Meaning of Repentance," *Brigham Young University 1984–85 Devotional and Fireside Speeches* (Provo, Utah: Brigham Young University, 1985), p. 96. An edited version of this address that was delivered at BYU on 26 March 1985 has been printed in the August 1988 *Ensign,* pp. 6–9.

8. James E. Talmage, *The Articles of Faith,* 50th ed. (Salt Lake City: The Church of Jesus Christ of Latter-day Saints, 1970), p. 109.

9. Spencer W. Kimball, *The Miracle of Forgiveness* (Salt Lake City: Bookcraft, 1969), p. 194.

10. Bruce C. Hafen, "Beauty for Ashes: The Atonement of Jesus Christ," unpublished transcript of an address delivered at the general session of the 1988 Religious Educators' Symposium on the New Testament, 11 August 1988, Brigham Young University, Provo, Utah, p. 12.

11. Orson Pratt, "True Repentance," chapter 2 in *A Series of Pamphlets by Orson Pratt* (Liverpool: Franklin D. Richards, 1852),

p. 17; reprinted in *Orson Pratt: Writings of an Apostle,* Republished by Jerry Burnett and Charles Pope (Salt Lake City: Mormon Heritage Publishers, 1976).

12. Robert L. Millet and Joseph Fielding McConkie, lectures on cassette tape, *Great Doctrines from the Book of Mormon* (Salt Lake City: Bookcraft, 1988).

13. Bruce R. McConkie, *Mormon Doctrine,* 2d ed. (Salt Lake City: Bookcraft, 1966), p. 60.

14. Bruce R. McConkie, "What Think Ye of Salvation by Grace?" *Brigham Young University 1983–84 Fireside and Devotional Speeches* (Provo, Utah: Brigham Young University, 1984), p. 48.

4

Confession: Attitudes and Actions

Not only did the Lord reveal to the Prophet Joseph Smith in this dispensation that confession was one of the indicators of true repentance (see D&C 58:43; 64:7) but also the Lord has throughout the sacred recorded history of mankind repeatedly taught the importance of confession to repentance. In the Book of Mormon the Lord told Alma to teach the people that "whosoever transgresseth against me, him shall ye judge according to the sins which he has committed; and if he confess his sins before thee and me, and repenteth in the sincerity of his heart, him shall ye forgive, and I will forgive him also" (Mosiah 26:29; see also verses 32–36; Moroni 6:7). In the Old Testament the author of the book of Proverbs understood this concept when he wrote, "He that covereth his sins shall not prosper, but whoso confesseth and forsaketh them shall have mercy" (Proverbs 28:13). Numerous other biblical passages teach the necessity of confession:

I acknowledged my sin unto thee, and mine iniquity have I not hid. I said, I will confess my transgressions unto the Lord; and thou forgavest the iniquity of my sin. (Psalm 32:5.)

If they shall confess their iniquity, and the iniquity of their fathers, with their trespass which they trespassed against me, and that also they have walked contrary unto me; . . . if then their uncircumcised hearts be humbled, and they then accept of the punishment of their iniquity:

Then will I remember my covenant with Jacob, and also my covenant with Isaac, and also my covenant with Abraham will I remember; and I will remember the land (Leviticus 26:40–42).

In addition to instructing God's children on the intrinsic role of confession in the repentance process, the Old Testament also records that formal public ritual was utilized to remind the Israelites of this essential principle. This was particularly evident under the law of Moses.

And if a soul sin . . . he shall confess that he hath sinned in that thing:

And he shall bring his trespass offering unto the Lord for his sin which he hath sinned . . . and the priest shall make an atonement for him concerning his sin. (Leviticus 5:1, 5–6.)

The confession and trespass offering were the *outward acknowledgment of sin*, which served to remind the transgressor of the *inner attitudes of penitence* which are indicative of true repentance. Each part of the animal sacrificed as a trespass offering was symbolic of a certain aspect of the sinner's personal life. Though it was a public confession, the ritual symbolized the inner thoughts, feelings, and affections of the heart of the man.[1]

The prophet Daniel's earnest, prayerful confession before the Lord on behalf of all Israel further teaches the humility and contrition of spirit that are essential to sincere confession.

And I set my face unto the Lord God, to seek by prayer and supplications, with fasting, and sackcloth, and ashes:

And I prayed unto the Lord my God, and made my confession, and said, O Lord, the great and dreadful God, keeping the covenant and mercy to them that love him and to them that keep his commandments;

We have sinned, and have committed iniquity, and have done wickedly, and have rebelled, even by departing from thy precepts. . . .

O Lord, hear; O Lord, forgive; O Lord, hearken and do. (Daniel 9:3–19.)

In the New Testament several scriptural statements also attest to the significance of confession as an integral part of repentance. The people who came to John the Baptist to partake of the ordinance of baptism were baptized only after they had confessed their sins and brought forth "fruits meet for repentance" (see Matthew 3:1–6). Even after the fulfillment of the law of Moses when many of the ritualistic requirements were done away, the Savior's Apostles continued to teach with clarity the necessity of confession. The Apostle James exhorted, "Confess your faults one to another, and pray one for another, that ye may be healed" (James 5:16). John, in his epistle to the Saints, wrote, "If we confess our sins, he is faithful and just to forgive us our sins, and to cleanse us from all unrighteousness" (1 John 1:9).

In another light, the New Testament also teaches that confession "unto righteousness" and salvation requires not only the confession of sins but also a confession (or acceptance) of Jesus as the Savior of the world. It was in this context that the Apostle Paul wrote to the Roman Saints: "For with the heart man believeth unto righteousness; and with the mouth confession is made unto salvation" (Romans 10:10). While it is clear from the context surrounding this passage that Paul was speaking of confessing the name of Christ "unto salvation," it is also possible to make a powerful application of his words to the doctrine of repentance. True repentance requires an *attitude* of confession in the heart as well as an *action* of confession coming from the mouth. This important principle is reflected in the dogma of virtually all Christian denominations, although there is great diversity in the specific applications and rituals of confession. Whether it be a private, personal confession of sins, confession to the clergy, or a more public confession to the congregation, the ritual or act of verbal confession serves merely as a *reminder* of what should be happening inside the soul of man. Confession is like a mirror whereby the sinner can examine himself spiritually and recognize his need for the cleansing power of Christ. Thus confession is an outward *action* that must mirror an inward *attitude*.

"Sorry After a Godly Manner": The Attitude of Confession

In the confession process the self-examination and acknowledgment of our sins and unworthiness should evoke in us a sense of spiritual sorrow and separation. The Apostle Paul spoke of this necessary sorrow of the soul when he declared to the Corinthian Saints:

> Now I rejoice, not that ye were made sorry, but that ye sorrowed to repentance, for ye were made sorry after a godly manner, that ye might receive damage by us in nothing.
>
> For godly sorrow worketh repentance to salvation not to be repented of: but the sorrow of the world worketh death. (2 Corinthians 7:9–10.)

This "godly sorrow" of which Paul spoke is the foundational attitude of confession. It is the indicator of true faith in Christ and the only genuine motivation for "bring[ing] forth fruits meet for repentance." Without godly sorrow there can be no repentance, for it is that which "worketh repentance to salvation."

Remorse Is Not Godly Sorrow

Paul spoke of a different kind of sorrow, one which "worketh death." He called it the sorrow of the world, which is the opposite of "godly sorrow." It is a sorrow for sins and circumstances that does not yield "fruits meet for repentance." Mormon described this condition in his own people as the "sorrowing of the damned."

> And it came to pass that when I, Mormon, saw their lamentation and their mourning and their sorrow before the Lord, my heart did begin to rejoice within me, knowing the mercies and the long-suffering of the Lord, therefore supposing that he would be merciful unto them that they would again become a righteous people.
>
> But behold this my joy was vain, for their sorrowing was not unto repentance, because of the goodness of God; but it was rather the sorrowing of the damned, because the Lord would not always suffer them to take happiness in sin.
>
> And they did not come unto Jesus with broken hearts and contrite spirits, but they did curse God, and wish to die. (Mormon 2:12–14.)

Mormon's tragic account of the spiritual decline of his people pointedly demonstrates that sorrow, regret, and remorse do not necessarily bring about repentance. Many are remorseful for past actions, and regret the consequences that have befallen them, but do nothing to change or to come unto Christ and comply with the requirements of the gospel. "Repentance is not that superficial sorrow felt by the wrongdoer when 'caught in the act'—a sorrow not for sin, but for sin's detection," wrote Elder Orson F. Whitney. "Chagrin is not repentance. Mortification and shame alone bring no change of heart toward right feeling and right living. Even remorse is not all there is to repentance."[2] Remorse, then, is to godly sorrow as belief is to faith. Belief can be passive, whereas true faith is a principle of action. James taught that faith requires action, whereas "the devils . . . believe, and tremble" (James 2:19). Devils may acknowledge the existence of God, but they exercise no "faith unto repentance." Similarly, "godly sorrow *worketh* repentance to salvation." Godly sorrow is an attitude of action which implies commitment to change. Elder Orson Pratt eloquently differentiated between mere remorse or regret and godly sorrow:

There are different kinds of sorrow. Thieves, rob-
bers, murderers, adulterers, etc., are frequently sorrowful because they have been detected in the crimes they
have committed. They are not sorrowful because they
have sinned against God, or because they have injured
others; but they are sorry because their crimes have
been exposed, or they have been prevented from a realization of the happiness which they anticipated. This is
the sorrow of the world; and it is of the same nature as
the sorrowing of the evil spirits in hell: they are sorry
when they fail to accomplish their malicious designs
against God and His people. This kind of sorrow worketh death.

Others have a species of sorrow arising through fear.
They are convinced that they have, in numerous instances, violated the law of God, and they greatly fear
the consequences in the great judgment day; but yet
they feel no disposition to reform. . . .

But the sorrow that is acceptable in the sight of God,
is that which leads to true repentance, or reformation of
conduct; it is the sorrow which arises not only through
fear of punishment, but through a proper sense of the
evil consequences of sin; it is that sorrow which arises
from a knowledge of our own unworthiness, and from
a contrast of our own degraded and fallen condition
with the mercy, goodness, and holiness of God. We are
sorry that we should ever have condescended to do
evil. We are sorry that we should ever have rendered
ourselves so unworthy before God; we are sorry at the
weakness of our own fallen nature. This kind of sorrow
will lead us to obey every commandment of God; it
will make us humble and childlike in our dispositions; it
will impart unto us meekness and lowliness of mind; it
will cause our hearts to be broken and our spirits to be
contrite; it will cause us to watch, with great careful-
ness, every word, thought, and deed; it will call up our
past dealings with mankind, and we will feel most anxious to make restitution to all whom we may have, in
any way, injured . . . these and many other good things

are the results of a Godly sorrow for sin. This is repentance not in word, but in deed: this is the sorrow with
which the heavens are pleased.[3]

A Broken Heart and a Contrite Spirit

While Paul used the term "godly sorrow" to characterize
that attitude that precedes and promotes actions of confession and repentance, the Book of Mormon calls it "a broken
heart and a contrite spirit." Both terms can be used inter-
changeably to teach the concept of God's sorrow—feeling
the sorrow for our sins that God would have us feel in order
to bring about our repentance and submission to him. Lehi
taught his son Jacob that Christ's atoning sacrifice was made
"to answer the ends of the law, unto all those who have a
broken heart and a contrite spirit; and unto none else can the
ends of the law be answered" (2 Nephi 2:7). The resurrected
Lord taught the Nephites they should no longer offer animal
sacrifices under the law of Moses. He commanded them instead to "offer for a sacrifice unto me a broken heart and a
contrite spirit. And whoso cometh unto me with a broken
heart and a contrite spirit, him will I baptize with fire and
with the Holy Ghost." (3 Nephi 9:19–20.) Several other passages in the Book of Mormon also refer to this attitude as one
that must accompany repentance and precede baptism (see 3
Nephi 12:19; Ether 4:15; Moroni 6:2).

The phrase "a broken heart and a contrite spirit" may be
synonymous, to a degree, with Paul's concept of "godly sorrow," but it also carries additional connotations. What exactly does it mean and how does it apply specifically to true
repentance? Elder Bruce R. McConkie wrote:

> To have a broken heart and a contrite spirit is to be
> broken down with deep sorrow for sin, to be humbly
> and thoroughly penitent, to have attained sincere and
> purposeful repentance. . . .
>
> This includes an honest, heartfelt contrition of soul,
> a contrition born of a broken heart and a contrite spirit.

It presupposes a frank, personal acknowledgment that one's acts have been evil in the sight of Him who is holy. There is no mental reservation in godly sorrow, no feeling that perhaps one's sins are not so gross or serious after all. It is certainly more than regret either because the sin has been brought to light or because some preferential reward or status has been lost because of it.[4]

The concepts implied in the phrase "a broken heart and a contrite spirit" encompass considerably more than just a repentant attitude. There are so many attributes and attitudes associated with it that it may be nearly impossible to fully define the terms. To better understand the relationship between a broken heart and a contrite spirit and confession, it is essential to emphasize two important elements of godly sorrow.

1. *An "awful awareness" of our unworthiness before God.* Before sinners can obtain a remission of sins they must experience something akin to what King Benjamin described as "an awful view of their own guilt and abominations, which doth cause them to shrink from the presence of the Lord" (Mosiah 3:25). This stark realization of guilt, King Benjamin told his people, awakens "you to a sense of your nothingness, and your worthless and fallen state" (Mosiah 4:5) and thus produces a broken heart wherein seeds of repentance can take root. This "awful awareness" must include a self-inflicted stripping away of all rationalization and self-justification. There is no room in a broken heart and a contrite spirit for making feeble excuses or blaming others for our sins. As Alma declared to his wayward son, Corianton: "Let your sins trouble you, with that trouble which shall bring you down unto repentance. . . . Do not endeavor to excuse yourself in the least point because of your sins, . . . but do you let the justice of God, and his mercy, and his long-suffering have full sway in your heart; and let it bring you down to the dust in humility." (Alma 42:29–30.) It is a profoundly painful view of ourselves as we "really are" (Jacob 4:13) and as God's all-penetrating eye sees us.

President Spencer W. Kimball declared:

> There must be a consciousness of guilt. It cannot be brushed aside. It must be acknowledged and not rationalized away. It must be given its full importance. . . .
>
> Rationalizing is the enemy to repentance. . . .
>
> The searing of one's conscience is certainly inimical to repentance, and to justify and rationalize is not the highway to repentance. . . . Someone has said, "Conscience is a celestial spark that God has put into every man for the purpose of saving his soul." It awakens the soul to consciousness of sin; it stimulates him to want to do better, to make adjustments, and to accept the sin in its full weight and size, to be willing to face facts and meet issues and pay penalties.[5]

Accompanying the "awful awareness" of unworthiness before the Lord is the yearning to be cleansed and to stand approved once again. It is much more than mere recognition of sin. It is a "sackcloth and ashes" humility that promotes spiritual growth and leads one to a condition described by President David O. McKay as a "change of nature befitting heaven."

> What progress can there be for a man unconscious of his faults? Such a man has lost the fundamental element of growth, which is the realization that there is something bigger, better, and more desirable than the condition in which he now finds himself. In the soil of self-satisfaction, true growth has poor nourishment. Its roots find greater succor in discontent. . . .
>
> The first step to knowledge is a realization of the lack of it; and the first step towards spiritual growth is the belief in a higher and better life, or conversely, a realization of the meanness of one's present state. Repentance is the turning away from that which is low and the striving for that which is higher. As a principle of salvation, it involves not only a desire for that which is better, but also a sorrow—not merely remorse—but true

sorrow for having become contaminated in any degree with things sinful. . . . [It] "is sorrow for sin with self-condemnation." . . . It is, therefore, more than mere remorse; "it comprehends a change of nature befitting heaven."[6]

2. Willing submission and surrender to God's will for us. Perhaps one of the most important indicators of godly sorrow for sin and contrition of the soul is a willingness to submit to whatever the Lord requires of us in order to obtain a remission of our sins. Not only did King Benjamin teach his people about the necessity of an "awful awareness" of their sinful state, but he also taught them that they must willingly and lovingly surrender themselves to the Lord. To overcome the "natural man" and obtain a remission of sins required that "they humble themselves and become as little children" (Mosiah 3:18). This means that a person who truly desires forgiveness yields "to the enticings of the Holy Spirit, and putteth off the natural man and becometh a saint through the atonement of Christ the Lord, and becometh as a child, submissive, meek, humble, patient, full of love, willing to submit to all things which the Lord seeth fit to inflict upon him" (Mosiah 3:19).

It is not uncommon for some who desire to repent, but whose hearts are not yet broken and whose spirits are less than contrite, to become selectively submissive. They desire to repent on *their* terms rather than on *his* terms. They want to make repentance easy, pain-free, and convenient when in reality it is difficult and demanding and may require humiliation, public embarrassment, pain, restrictions, or inconvenience. It is not "godly sorrow" but "selective submission" when an individual:

- Confesses a major sin to the appropriate priesthood leader, but is unwilling to follow the counsel or prescription he receives.
- Procrastinates his confession and repentance until he gets into the mission field so he will not be embarrassed at home by having to wait a little longer before he can serve.

- Resents the restriction to not partake of the sacrament because he is worried about what others might think or that he might suffer a degree of personal embarrassment.
- Disguises the severity of his sin in his confession to his priesthood leader so that he may be accepted to or avoid being expelled from a Church-owned university or college.

In a similar vein, President Spencer W. Kimball often applied a verbal test to determine the "depth of one's conviction of sin." His questions can serve as an inventory of our own willingness to submit:

> Do you wish to be forgiven?
>
> Could you accept excommunication for the sin if deemed necessary? Why do you feel you should not be excommunicated? If you were, would you become bitter at the Church and its officers? Would you cease your activities in the Church? Would you work your way back to baptism and restoration of former blessings even through years? . . .
>
> Have you told your [spouse] or parents? Have you confessed your total sins?
>
> Are you humble now? Is it the result of "being forced to be humble"?
>
> Have you wrestled with your problems as did Enos? Has your soul hungered for your soul's sake?[7]

The extent to which our heart is broken and our spirit contrite will largely be determined by what we are willing to do to have that burden lifted from our sin-weary shoulders. If our answers are tentative or qualified we have not yet fully experienced that "godly sorrow [which] worketh repentance" (2 Corinthians 7:10). "There can be no conditions attached to unconditional surrender to God," wrote Elder Neal A. Maxwell. "Unconditional surrender means we cannot keep our obsessions, possessions, or cheering constituencies. . . . Every obsession or preoccupation must give way in total submission."[8] If we truly possess the proper attitude of confession, our hearts will be broken with a piercing sorrow for sin and an "awful awareness" of our unworthiness. Our spirits will be contrite and we will desire to submit to God's will and be taught what we must do to obtain a remission of our sins. Only when this occurs can we begin to come out of the "hole" into which we have dug ourselves through sin. C. S. Lewis insightfully observed:

> Fallen man is not simply an imperfect creature who needs improvement: he is a rebel who must lay down his arms. Laying down your arms, surrendering, saying you're sorry, realising that you have been on the wrong track and getting ready to start life over again from the ground floor—that is the only way out of a "hole." This process of surrender . . . is what Christians call repentance. Now repentance is no fun at all. It is something much harder than merely eating humble pie. It means unlearning all the self-conceit and self-will that we have been training ourselves into. . . . It means killing part of yourself, undergoing a kind of death. . . .
>
> Remember, this repentance, this willing submission to humiliation and a kind of death, is not something God demands of you before He will take you back and which He could let you off if He chose: it is simply a description of what going back to Him is like.[9]

How Is "Godly Sorrow" Obtained?

A student posed to me an important, thoughtful question. "What can you do, if anything, to obtain that kind of godly sorrow? What if you don't feel genuinely sorry for your sins? Can you still repent?" As I pondered those questions I could think of numerous examples of people with whom I had counseled who really felt no remorse, let alone godly sorrow, for their sins. I had heard confessions from some who knew they were to confess, who desired to be worthy of temple recommends, and who were willing to make the necessary amends and adjustments in their lives, but who had a noticeable lack of the attitude of confession—the broken heart and the contrite spirit. Since there cannot be true repentance without it, I wondered what I could do as a bishop to help them feel that godly sorrow.

As I struggled with this dilemma, and as my heart went out to those in such a circumstance, I learned that there really wasn't anything that *I* could do to bring them to that desired state. There is no easy program of prescribed steps that leads to godly sorrow. The Spirit testified to me that godly sorrow, like charity, is a spiritual gift. It is bestowed upon us through our faith in Christ. "Godly sorrow is born of the Spirit," wrote Elder Bruce R. McConkie. "It is a gift of God that comes to those who have a broken heart and a contrite spirit."[10] In his classic sermon to his people on the pure love of Christ—defined as charity—Mormon wrote: "Wherefore, my beloved brethren, *pray unto the Father with all the energy of heart,* that ye may be filled with this love, which he hath bestowed upon all who are true followers of his Son, Jesus Christ" (Moroni 7:48; italics added). Godly sorrow, like charity, comes as a spiritual endowment to assist in our repentance. When we, "with full purpose of heart, acting no hypocrisy and no deception before God, but with real intent" (2 Nephi 31:13), "pray unto the Father with all the energy of heart," we will be filled with the godly sorrow that the Lord desires us to feel. We must plead with him to teach us what we must feel *and* do—for he alone dispenses the correct dosage of godly sorrow and knows the proper prescription to soothe our spiritual sores and heal our broken hearts.

"I Will Confess My Sins": The Action of Confession

To focus on the *action* of confession in the absence of the *attitude* of confession would be to view it merely as another "step" in the "checklist" of repentance, rather than as a natural outgrowth of godly sorrow. Questions such as "Do I have to confess my sins? What sins must I confess? To whom should I confess?" may reflect this overemphasis on the action of confession at the expense of the attitude. When our hearts are broken and our spirits contrite, the subsequent desire to "set things right" will lead us toward following the Spirit and away from groping for the letter of the law.

The scriptures speak of two major acts of confession. Alma taught that sins were to be confessed both to the Lord and his anointed representative (see Mosiah 26:29). In this dispensation the Lord reaffirmed that sins were to be confessed "unto thy brethren, and before the Lord" (D&C 59:12). Commenting on this passage in relation to major sins, President Spencer W. Kimball declared: "It is plain that there are two confessions to make: one to the Lord and the other to 'the brethren,' meaning the proper ecclesiastical officers."[11] It is significant that two confessions are prescribed by the Lord for the forgiveness of sins. Elder Bruce R. McConkie explained the significance:

> There are thus two confessions and two sources of forgiveness. A sinner must always confess all sins, great and small, to the Lord; in addition, any sins involving moral turpitude and any serious sins for which a person might be disfellowshipped or excommunicated must also be confessed to the Lord's agent, who in most instances is the bishop. The bishop is empowered to forgive sins as far as the Church is concerned, meaning that he can choose to retain the repentant person in full fellowship and not impose court penalties upon him. Ultimate forgiveness in all instances and for all sins comes from the Lord and from the Lord only.[12]

With the "awful awareness" of our sins that accompanies a broken heart, we will keenly feel the need to come before the Lord in complete confession. Such confession results from our yearning to be healed of our sins and restored to the Lord. It should not come out of fear or from a shallow sense of obligation to perform a "checklist repentance." With the "wilful submission to the Lord" that characterizes a contrite spirit, we will be prompted and prodded by the workings of the spirit to approach the proper priesthood leader, as necessary, in humble confession and to receive of his counsel and support. Under such conditions the necessary *action* of confession, as a fruit of the *attitude* of confession, becomes a blessing rather than a burden.

Confession Is More than Disclosure

Psychologists and counselors would agree that confession as disclosure, followed by the open discussion of one's innermost feelings, is essential to emotional healing and proper mental health. In the spiritual sense, however, confession is much more than catharsis. If the issue were our mental and emotional welfare alone, then it would be helpful to confess our sins, discuss our problems, and bare our souls to almost anyone who would lend a listening and compassionate ear. The scriptures and the prophets, however, make it clear that our confession should be made in all cases to the Lord and under certain circumstances to the judge in Israel. Why is this so? The answer is found in the knowledge that confession in the spirit of repentance is much more than the revealing of deeds. If disclosure alone were what the Lord desired, we would not need to admit our sins and innermost feelings to God, since in his omniscience he would already know them. Likewise, under such a premise it would only be necessary to disclose to the designated priesthood leader those sins of which he was unaware. Confession to the Lord or to a judge in Israel is not just telling them *what they need to know*. It is the expression of a commitment or making of a covenant with them concerning *what we are going to do*. Full disclosure of our sins remains an incomplete confession unless it leads to two higher and more important purposes.

1. Confession as a covenant. For our own benefit, we disclose our deeds to the Lord, even though he already knows them, and to priesthood leaders, who may or may not know them. Such open acknowledgment of our evil actions promotes a spirit of humility and a desire to change. Confession is our opportunity to vow to make the necessary adjustments in our lives. Disclosure without commitment to change does not guarantee any enduring effects. It is only through the observance of a solemn covenant which should go hand in hand with confession that a remission of sins and peace of conscience can result. Elder Orson Pratt observed:

> Though we may break off from our sins, and reform our conduct, yet we cannot expect a forgiveness of our past sins without humble confession. . . . This confession should be accompanied with a *promise and determination to sin no more.* To confess our sins before God, would be of no particular benefit, unless we were determined to forsake them. *Without a covenant or promise before God, that we will forsake sin with an unshaken determination, that we will henceforth yield to no evil, our confession and repentance will be vain,* and we must not expect to be pardoned; for the Holy One of Israel cannot be deceived, and will not pardon those who merely confess their sins, and still make no resolution to forsake them; *a confession of sins, unaccompanied with the resolution to forsake, is solemn mockery before Him,* and will add to our guilt, and increase the displeasure of heaven against us. . . . Such a confession must be accompanied with a solemn covenant or promise to sin no more; and the heart should be fixed and immovable in that covenant.[13]

2. Confession as an opportunity to receive help and direction. Confessing sins to friends, roommates, or even family members may seem a valuable emotional release. There may even be a temporary lifting of the heavy mental burden, but even this feeling is fleeting. The lasting healing of both mind and spirit can only come from the Great Physician. When we "cast our burdens upon the Lord" through a complete confession and a commitment to forsake sin, we are then in a position to be taught by the Master. His guidance far surpasses any emotional lift or well-meant advice received from mere mortals. Christ can give divine direction to our suffering souls because, as Paul said, since "he himself hath suffered being tempted, he is able to succour them that are tempted. . . . [He] was in all points tempted like as we are, yet without sin. Let us therefore come boldly unto the throne of grace . . . and find grace to help in time of need." (Hebrews 2:18; 4:15–16.) We can plead with the Lord to instruct us as to what we must now do to fully repent and we can petition him for the strength and courage to do it. In answer to our humble solicitation the Spirit will direct us in our journey along the path of true repentance.

> Likewise the Spirit also helpeth our infirmities: for we know not what we should pray for as we ought: but the Spirit itself maketh intercession for us with groanings which cannot be uttered.
>
> And he that searcheth the hearts knoweth what is the mind of the Spirit, because he maketh intercession for the saints according to the will of God. (Romans 8:26–27.)

Just as God, through the intercession of the Spirit, can provide infinitely superior spiritual guidance for a transgressor, so it is with those priesthood leaders who are designated as common judges in Israel. Common judges in Israel (bishops, branch presidents, mission presidents, stake presidents) have been ordained and set apart to a special stewardship which uniquely qualifies and spiritually empowers them to lift the burdens of those who confess major sins — especially those sins that may affect Church membership. These inspired priesthood leaders, regardless of background or station in life, can provide the confessor with the counsel and direction needed in the repentance process. No friend or family member, regardless of his or her wise counsel or personal compassion, can supplant this divinely authorized spiritual guidance or usurp this unique priesthood responsibility. Judges in Israel alone hold the special priesthood keys and the powers of discernment which enable them to receive confessions, give inspired instruction, and dispense the necessary discipline that may lead the transgressor to an ultimate forgiveness. Elder Boyd K. Packer affirms that this kind of inspired guidance and direction comes from the Lord through the proper priesthood channels.

> The Lord has set up some precise channels in the Church, and He invariably extends inspiration through

these channels. However, we are often guilty of an "end run" to someone [other than those in the proper channel]. . . . While we do not always follow the proper channels of authority and while we sometimes preempt responsibility that belongs. . . . to a bishop, the Lord invariably stays in channel. He will not yield revelation and inspiration to us when we are out of those channels.[14]

> Know then . . . that there is a great cleansing power. And know that you can be clean.
> . . . For those of you inside the Church there is a way, not entirely painless, but certainly possible. You can stand clean and spotless before Him. Guilt will be gone, and you can be at peace. Go to your bishop. He holds the key to this cleansing power.[15]

Although confession does require "sackcloth and ashes" humility and a degree of personal embarrassment, it should not be dreaded or dodged. A seriously ill patient, though uncertain of the treatment and the outcome, looks with trust rather than trepidation to the care of a competent doctor. How unwise it would be for a person who is diagnosed early with a potentially life-threatening disease to postpone treatments until he begins to feel unbearable pain! Similarly a person guilty of a major transgression must not delay his confession to the proper priesthood leader because he may not yet fully feel godly sorrow. Such a postponement may actually cause him to forfeit the guidance and direction that could precipitate the broken heart and contrite spirit needed to fully repent. Complete and contrite confession to the Lord and to the judge in Israel for serious sins is the means whereby spiritually sick souls can receive a potent prescription dispensed with compassion and concern for their ultimate healing and regeneration.

Sometimes the medicine prescribed comes in the form of official Church discipline. Unless our repentance has included "a broken heart and a contrite spirit" we may view this discipline as harsh or "difficult to swallow." Those who misunderstand its purpose may view excommunication, disfellowshipment, or other formal restrictions as unfairly punitive and humiliating. On the contrary, Elder Theodore M. Burton noted that "the most loving action the Church can take at times is to disfellowship or excommunicate a person."[16] When deemed necessary through inspiration, these repentance remedies can help the sinner fully realize the seriousness of his transgression. If a serious offense is treated too lightly it is more likely to be repeated. Such Church actions can ensure that the necessary price for repentance is paid. They also serve to mercifully protect the errant person from the full weight and responsibility of his covenants, which if left in full force would bring condemnation upon him in his yet unforgiven state. Through Church discipline a wrongdoer can demonstrate to the Lord, to the Church, and to others a sincere desire to repent and be forgiven whatever the cost. This period of discipline is an opportunity to be retrained as a *disciple* of him who made our repentance possible. Finally, even if it accomplishes nothing for the sinner it preserves the purity and integrity of the Church.

Confession to Others

In addition to the required confessions already discussed, the Lord has stipulated that confessing our sins to others may sometimes also be necessary. James wrote, "Confess your faults one to another, and pray one for another, that ye may be healed" (James 5:16). In this dispensation the Lord revealed to the Prophet Joseph the "law of the Church," found in Doctrine and Covenants section 42. Included in this law were instructions for dealing with transgressors. Part of those instructions called for confessions, both public and private, to those people who had been offended or harmed by the sinner's misdeed. "If any shall offend in secret," declared the Lord, "he or she shall be rebuked in secret, that he or she may have opportunity to confess in secret to him or her whom he or she has offended, and to God that the church may not speak reproachfully of him or her" (D&C 42:92).

The Lord established this "law" of confession to others not simply because he wanted us to unveil our sins and seek the forgiveness of those who may have been adversely affected. He wanted this type of confession, like confession to God and to priesthood leaders, to be an opportunity for recommitment, restoration of personal integrity, and rebuilding of relationships. "When one has wronged another in deep transgression or in injuries of lesser magnitude," wrote President Spencer W. Kimball, "he, the aggressor, who gave the offense . . . should immediately make amends by confessing to the injured one and doing all in his power to clear up the matter and again establish good feelings between the parties."[17]

This principle of confession to others, as outlined in the scriptures and reemphasized by prophets, is sometimes misunderstood by those who unwisely and unnecessarily confess their wrongs to others. President Brigham Young cautioned against this type of counterproductive confession:

> I believe in coming out and being plain and honest with that which should be made public, and in keeping to yourselves that which should be kept. If you have your weaknesses, keep them hid from your brethren as much as you can. You never hear me ask the people to tell their follies. . . . Tell to the public that which belongs to the public. If you have sinned against the people, confess to them. If you have sinned against a family or a neighbourhood, go to them and confess. If you have sinned against your Ward, confess to your Ward. If you have sinned against one individual, take that person by yourselves and make your confession to him. And if you have sinned against your God, or against yourselves, confess to God, and keep the matter to yourselves, for I do not want to know anything about it. . . .
>
> Keep your follies that do not concern others to yourselves, and keep your private wickedness as still as possible; hide it from the eyes of the public gaze as far as you can. . . . We wish to see people honestly confess *as they should* and *what they should.*[18]

There is no easy or fail-safe formula which delineates exactly how, when, what, and under which circumstances we should confess to our fellowmen. Sometimes the situation may be simple and clear-cut and we may know exactly what to do in order to restore our integrity and obtain forgiveness from those we have wronged. Other situations, however, may make such confession unwise and counterproductive. Some attempts at confession or reconciliation could actually inflict unnecessary spiritual and emotional wounds, further exacerbate problems, or even interfere with the restorative repentance process. Under other circumstances it may actually be impossible to confess our wrongs to those whom we have offended. While it is true that some may not make enough effort to confess their sins to those they have harmed, there are also those who, almost in a spirit of self-flagellation, become preoccupied with confessing to others. This preoccupation may range from the unwise confessing of sins to anyone who will listen to unnecessary worrying and fretting about confessing every little infraction.

With these types of self-punishing behaviors, roadblocks to repentance are unnecessarily erected. For these reasons we must remember that the Lord, in his infinite love and compassion, desires us to repent—to be healed of our sin-induced sickness and to have the burdensome load lifted. "Christ came to lift us up, not put us down," declared Elder Paul H. Dunn.[19] Our confession to others, then, should be guided by promptings of the Spirit of the Lord. He knows what is best for us and will teach us through the power of the Holy Ghost and through the inspired counsel of the common judges in Israel what we must do. If we will follow this guidance, we will not become bogged down with unnecessary anxiety in our repentance process.

Is That All There Is?

Several years ago the Church Educational System produced an impressive filmstrip entitled "Remembered No More," which was used in seminary classes throughout the Church. This instructive and inspiring filmstrip contained no dialogue—merely pictures and music. Through unique

camera angles and moving music the viewers could almost
feel the godly sorrow of a young man as he made an agoniz-
ing effort to confess to his bishop. In addition to depicting
the emotional struggle and the difficulty of confession, the
filmstrip also showed an inspired bishop teaching this young
man about the meaning of repentance and its relationship to
the atonement of Christ. As the filmstrip ended the young
man left the bishop's office visibly happier than before he entered—as if an enormous burden had been lifted from his
shoulders.

This powerful filmstrip did much good in teaching seminary students the proper role of confession. However, some
students may have missed the total message and assumed that
as the happy young man left the bishop's office his repentance was complete. "Is that all there is to repentance?" some
may have asked silently. Godly sorrow coupled with proper
confession does bring a sense of relief and freedom. President
Spencer W. Kimball wrote:

> Confession brings peace. How often have people de-
> parted from my office relieved and lighter of heart than
> for a long time! Their burdens were lighter, having been
> shared. They were free. The truth had made them free.
> . . . There is substantial psychological strength in con-
> fession. . . . One lifts at least part of his burden and
> places it on other shoulders which are able and willing
> to help carry the load. Then there comes [a sense of]
> satisfaction in having taken another step in doing all
> that is possible to rid oneself of the burden of transgres-
> sion.[20]

As difficult yet helpful and healing as confession is, it is
not the conclusion of the repentance process required by the
Lord. Through the *attitude* of confession—godly sorrow—
we open the gate; through the *action* of confession we step
onto the "strait and narrow path" leading to forgiveness.
Nephi's question serves as a guide to us: "And now, my beloved brethren [and sisters], after ye have gotten into this
strait and narrow path, I would ask if all is done? Behold, I say
unto you, Nay; for ye have not come thus far save it were by

the word of Christ with unshaken faith in him." (2 Nephi 31:19.) Repentance is not yet complete without the fulfillment of the second indicator designated by the Lord as the means whereby "ye may know if a man repenteth of his sins —behold, he will *confess* them and *forsake* them" (D&C 58:43; italics added). As essential as confession is, the culmination and final test of true repentance is in the forsaking of sin.

Notes

1. "Sacrifices and Offerings," Old Testament Slide Set L narration (Salt Lake City: Church Educational System, 1980), pp. 9–11.

2. Orson F. Whitney as quoted in *Latter-day Prophets and the Doctrine and Covenants*, compiled by Roy W. Doxey (Salt Lake City: Deseret Book Co., 1978), vol. 2, p. 240.

3. Orson Pratt, "True Repentance," *A Series of Pamphlets by Orson Pratt* (Liverpool: Franklin D. Richards, 1852), pp. 30–31; republished in *Orson Pratt: Writings of an Apostle* (Salt Lake City: Mormon Heritage Publishers, 1976).

4. Bruce R. McConkie, *Mormon Doctrine*, 2d ed. (Salt Lake City: Bookcraft, 1966), pp. 161, 292.

5. Spencer W. Kimball, "What Is True Repentance?" *New Era* May 1974, pp. 4–5.

6. David O. McKay, *Gospel Ideals* (Salt Lake City: The Improvement Era, 1953), pp. 12–13.

7. Spencer W. Kimball, *The Miracle of Forgiveness* (Salt Lake City: Bookcraft, 1969), pp. 160–61.

8. Neal A. Maxwell, *"Not My Will, But Thine"* (Salt Lake City: Bookcraft, 1988), pp. 92–93.

9. C. S. Lewis, *Mere Christianity* (London: Collins Fount, 1960), pp. 59–60.

10. Bruce R. McConkie, *A New Witness for the Articles of Faith* (Salt Lake City: Deseret Book Co., 1985), p. 235.

11. Spencer W. Kimball, *The Miracle of Forgiveness,* pp. 179–80.

12. Bruce R. McConkie, *A New Witness for the Articles of Faith,* p. 236.

13. Orson Pratt, "True Repentance," *A Series of Pamphlets by Orson Pratt,* pp. 31–32; italics added.

14. Boyd K. Packer, *Teach Ye Diligently* (Salt Lake City: Deseret Book Co., 1975), pp. 192–93.

15. Boyd K. Packer, Conference Report, April 1972, p. 138.

16. Theodore M. Burton, "To Forgive Is Divine," *Ensign*, May 1983, p. 70.

17. Spencer W. Kimball, *The Miracle of Forgiveness,* p. 186.

18. Brigham Young, *Journal of Discourses*, 8:362; italics added.

19. Paul H. Dunn, "By Faith and Hope, All Things Are Fulfilled," *Ensign*, May 1987, p. 75.

20. Spencer W. Kimball, *The Miracle of Forgiveness*, pp. 187–88.

5

Forsaking Sin:
The "Mighty Change"

It is plainly stated in the scriptures, both in ancient and modern dispensations, that confession must be accompanied by the forsaking of sin (see Proverbs 28:13; D&C 58:43). This integral component of repentance is all too often misunderstood to mean that one merely stops committing the particular sin of which he is repenting. The ceasing of one designated sin at a time is necessary and is certainly one element of forsaking, but to view the scriptural concept of forsaking sin only by this narrow and compartmentalized definition may rob us of a complete perspective of the true nature of repentance. The Lord's definition of forsaking implies the abandonment of sinfulness in every aspect of our lives and character. Without this broader meaning, forsaking becomes fragmented, as seen in the following two examples:

1. A person confesses a major moral transgression to his priesthood leader and promises to never again fall to *that*

transgression, but continues to blatantly disregard the Word of Wisdom by drinking or indulging in illicit drug use.

2. Another person confesses a sin of shoplifting. She forsakes *that* sin of stealing, seeks the forgiveness of the Lord and of the person offended. She even pays back the monetary value of the items taken. She abandons shoplifting, but continues her willful and malicious practice of "robbing" the good names of members of her ward through gossip, backbiting, and criticism.

In each of these examples it is apparent that while the individuals may have "forsaken" one specific sin or sinful situation, they really have not yet changed their disposition to sin. Each was attempting to give up one sin while clinging tenaciously to others. In some ways Isaiah's description of wickedness applies in such circumstances: "Woe unto them that draw iniquity with cords of vanity, and sin as it were with a cart rope" (Isaiah 5:18). Occasionally we cut the cords of vanity and let go of a favorite sin, but all too often in our "fragmentary forsaking" we merely cast sins off from the cart periodically rather than just letting go of the cart rope. President Spencer W. Kimball has declared that there is no true repentance if we only forsake some selected sins but continue to embrace sinfulness.

> That transgressor is not fully repentant who neglects his tithing, misses his meetings, breaks the Sabbath, fails in his family prayers, does not sustain the authorities of the Church, breaks the Word of Wisdom, does not love the Lord nor his fellowmen. A reforming adulterer who drinks or curses is not repentant. The repenting burglar who has sex play is not ready for forgiveness. God cannot forgive unless the transgressor shows a true repentance which spreads to all areas of his life.[1]

In contrast to those examples of "fragmentary forsaking," King Lamoni's father reflected the proper perspective of forsaking as an element of genuine repentance when he declared: "I will give away *all my sins* to know thee . . . and be saved at the last day" (Alma 22:18; italics added). His forsaking of sin was not selective, but total surrender. This comprehensive view of forsaking sin was articulated well by President Joseph F. Smith:

> True repentance is not only sorrow for sins, and humble penitence and contrition before God, but it involves the necessity of turning away from them, a discontinuance of all evil practices and deeds, a thorough reformation of life, a vital change from evil to good, from vice to virtue, from darkness to light.[2]

Forsaking, like confession, is comprised of attitudes as well as actions. It is not just the abandonment of an action — it is the changing of one's entire being. Alma aptly characterized this mortal metamorphosis as a "mighty change in your hearts" that causes a person to "sing the song of redeeming love" (see Alma 5:14, 26). Mere "fragmentary forsaking" falls far short of "a mighty change." It is this latter definition of forsaking that ultimately alters *both* the behavior and the being. Forsaking, as an indicator of true repentance, involves a "mighty change" of heart *and* a "mighty change" of direction and devotion.

A "Mighty Change" of Heart

Through the Old Testament prophet Ezekiel the Lord declared that there must be an abandonment of the overall desire for sinfulness and a change of heart and spirit.

> Repent, and turn yourselves from all your transgressions; so iniquity shall not be your ruin.
>
> Cast away from you all your transgressions, whereby ye have transgressed; and make you a new heart and a new spirit. (Ezekiel 18:30–31.)

Later the Lord again told the house of Israel that if they would indeed abandon their wicked desires, he would perform a great miracle in their behalf that would bring about a newness of attitude, character, and being.

Then will I sprinkle clean water upon you, and ye shall be clean: from all your filthiness, and from all your idols, will I cleanse you.

A new heart also will I give you, and a new spirit will I put within you: and I will take away the stony heart out of your flesh, and I will give you an heart of flesh.

And I will put my spirit within you, and cause you to walk in my statutes, and ye shall keep my judgments, and do them. (Ezekiel 36:25–27.)

Centuries later the Apostle Paul taught that repentance involved a total reformation. He explained that it implied such a mighty change of heart that a person actually becomes a "new creature" (see 2 Corinthians 5:17). Through the exercise of our "faith unto repentance" our old ways of evil become "crucified" with Christ and we begin to "walk in newness of life" (see Romans 6:2–6). Both Ezekiel and Paul emphasize that this mighty change of heart—this metamorphosis from the "old man" of sin to a "new man" which God has "created in righteousness and true holiness" (see Ephesians 4:24)—comes as a gift to us through the grace and mercy of Jesus Christ. The scriptures and prophets of God have declared that this mighty change, though a gift of grace, is bestowed upon us through the exercise of our own faith whereby we bring forth "fruits meet for repentance."

This combination of our own efforts to change and the spiritual renewal that comes as a merciful and loving gift from God constitutes the true meaning of forsaking sin. The Lamanite prophet Samuel held up the works of the repentant and faithful Lamanites as an example to the wicked Nephites of the merciful chastening of the Lord. He explained that his Lamanite brethren had been "led to believe the holy scriptures, yea, the prophecies of the holy prophets, which are written, which leadeth them to faith on the Lord, and unto repentance, which faith *and* repentance bringeth a change of heart unto them (Helaman 15:7; italics added).

This blending of man's faith and works with God's grace is reflected in the Greek word *metanoia*, which is translated as "repentance" in the New Testament. The definition of *metanoia* encompasses much more than just a change of behavior. It involves a change of thoughts, attitudes, and desires. It literally means "afterthought" or "change of mind," but it also implies complete conversion.

> It [*metanoia* or repentance] demands radical conversion, a transformation of nature, a definitive turning from evil, a resolute turning to God in total obedience (Mk. 1:15; Mt. 4:17; 18:3). . . . There can be no going back, only advance in responsible movement along the way now taken. It affects the whole man, first and basically the centre of personal life, then logically his conduct at all times and in all situations, his thoughts, words and acts (Mt. 12:33ff. par.; 23:26; Mk. 7:15 par.) . . . [It] is a proclamation of unconditional turning to God, or unconditional turning from all that is against God, not merely that which is downright evil, but that which in a given case makes total turning to God impossible (Mt. 5:29f., 44; 6:19f.; 7:13f. par.; 10:32–39 par.; Mk. 3:31ff. par.; Lk. 14:33, cf. Mk. 10:21 par.).[3]

Further implicit in this definition and commentary is the fact that a conscientious relinquishing of sin must be combined with a determined shunning of the trappings of sinfulness that may distract us from the required spiritual surrender to God. It is not just "afterthought" or a change of mind. *Meta* means "above" or "higher" as well as "after." We must evolve from a lower way of thinking and acting to a higher one in which our thoughts, desires, and attitudes coincide with the mind of Christ. Perhaps some other Rs that must not be overlooked in the repentance process are a *reeducation* of our mind, a *reordering* of our priorities, a *redirecting* of our desires, and a *reshaping* of our character. *Metanoia*, as Elder Theodore M. Burton declared, "means a change of mind or thought or thinking so powerful and so strong that it changes our very way of life."[4] This type of new heart, mind, and lifestyle was described by the Apostle Peter as "the divine nature." Peter invited us to become "partakers of the divine nature" by leaving behind the lusts of the world and doing instead those things that reflect the mind of Christ.

> Giving all diligence, add to your faith virtue; and to virtue knowledge;
> And to knowledge temperance [self-control]; and to temperance patience; and to patience godliness;
> And to godliness brotherly kindness; and to brotherly kindness charity.
> For if these things be in you, and abound, they make you that ye shall neither be barren nor unfruitful in the knowledge of our Lord Jesus Christ. (2 Peter 1:4–8.)

Peter then noted that "he that lacketh these things is blind . . . and hath forgotten that he was purged from his old sins" (2 Peter 1:9). In other words, his repentance is not of efficacy because his sinful nature remains unchanged.

President Spencer W. Kimball further declared that the mighty change of heart may also necessarily include a change of friends and associations, a change of circumstances and environments. "There must be an abandonment of the transgression. It must be genuine and consistent and continuing," he added. "And a temporary, momentary change of life is not sufficient." For people to truly forsake their evil doings they must "make changes in their lives, transformation in their habits, and . . . add new thoughts to their minds."[5] President Kimball also cautioned, "True repentance incorporates within it a washing, a purging, a changing of attitudes, a reappraising, a strengthening toward self-mastery. It is not a simple matter for one to transform his life overnight, nor to change attitudes in a moment, nor to rid himself in a hurry of unworthy companions."[6]

Thus true repentance is a serious and demanding process, and once we have committed ourselves there can be no hesitating. We must not attempt to straddle the imaginary line of demarcation between good and evil. "Ye cannot serve God and mammon," declared Jesus (Matthew 6:24). Such divided loyalties block the development of the faith required to forsake sin. We cannot, figuratively speaking, have one hand reaching for the fruit of the "tree of life" yet continue to dance and dine in the "great and spacious building," for it requires both hands and our whole heart and soul to cling to the "iron rod" (see 1 Nephi 11:8–36).

The Apostle Paul often taught the Saints through his many epistles about the thorough metamorphosis of life needed to become "new creatures." Newer translations and versions of the Bible elaborate on this teaching and may give a clearer view of the scope of this necessary transformation. "Therefore put to death whatever in your nature belongs to the earth —immorality, impurity, passion, desire, and greediness" (Colossians 3:2–5, Modern Language Edition). "But now is the time to cast off and throw away all these rotten garments of anger, hatred, cursing, and dirty language. Don't tell lies to each other; it was your old life with its wickedness that did that sort of thing; now it is dead and gone. You are living a brand new kind of life" (Colossians 3:8–10, Living Bible Edition). To the Thessalonians he wrote that they must even "abstain from all appearance of evil" (1 Thessalonians 5:22). The Ephesians he admonished, "Live no longer as the unsaved [unrepentant] do, for they are blinded and confused. Their closed hearts are full of darkness. . . . They don't care anymore about right and wrong. . . . Now your attitudes and thoughts must all be constantly changing for the better. Yes, you must be a new and different person, holy and good. Clothe yourself with this new nature." (Ephesians 4:17–19, 23–24; Living Bible Edition.)

It is clear from Paul's statements that to be truly repentant and forsake evil we must become different, in a positive and righteous way, from the people of the world—doing different deeds, thinking different thoughts, and practicing principles of righteousness. "Our lives must be better than they have ever been before," declared Elder Dean L. Larsen. "This simply means that we will become increasingly different from those around us whose lives follow the world's way. . . . We must clearly understand that it is not safe to move in the same direction the world is moving, even though we remain slightly behind the pace they set. Such a course will eventually lead us to the same problems and heartaches."[7]

While we may work to incorporate the necessary changes cited by the ancient and modern prophets, we cannot of ourselves attain the "mighty change" of heart. It comes to us as God's gift of grace as we exercise faith and diligence and, as Nephi declared, "after all we can do" (2 Nephi 25:23). Our own efforts will produce only an incomplete or temporary change of life without this gift of the Spirit made possible through the atonement of Jesus Christ. President Ezra Taft Benson wrote that many in the world "demonstrate great will-power and self-discipline in overcoming bad habits and weaknesses of the flesh. Yet at the same time they give no thought to the Master, sometimes even openly rejecting Him. Such changes of behavior, even if in a positive direction, do not constitute true repentance."[8] Often we, like those spoken of by President Benson, struggle mightily, even with the best of intentions, trying to overcome our carnal ways through our own efforts. We may feel overwhelmed and frustrated and hopelessly unable to change when we think we must rely solely on our puny human willpower. We can never achieve repentance in this way. However, if through our faith and works we are endowed with the "mighty change" of heart, we will find the desires to do evil purged from us by the power of the Holy Ghost, and the task of becoming a "new creature" will become infinitely easier. Elder Orson Pratt eloquently explained:

> The Holy Ghost [changes us] more thoroughly by renewing the inner man, and by purifying the affections, desires, and thoughts which have so long been habituated in the impure ways of sin. Without the aid of the Holy Ghost, a person who has long been accustomed to love sin, and whose affections and desires have long run with delight in the degraded channel of vice, would have but very little power to change his mind, at once, from its habituated course and walk, and to walk in newness of life. Though his sins may have been cleansed away, yet so great is the force of habit, that he would, without being renewed by the Holy Ghost, be easily overcome, and contaminated again by sin. Hence, it is infinitely important that the affections and desires

Then goeth he, and taketh to him seven other spirits more wicked than himself; and they enter in, and dwell there: and the last state of that man is worse than the first. (Luke 11:24–26.)

Although the "house" had been swept or cleansed, the evil spirit (and his additional cohorts) returned to the unoccupied house and reentered. In a similar way, our lives may be like the empty house after our sins are swept away. We remain vulnerable to a reinvasion of all manner of temptations and trouble if our lives are not filled up with renewed acts of righteousness, greater devotion to God, and increased service to others. We must become so filled with goodness that there is no room for our "former sins [to] return" (see D&C 82:7). As Elder Boyd K. Packer counseled:

Do not try merely to *discard* a bad habit or a bad thought. *Replace* it. When you try to eliminate a bad habit, if the spot where it used to be is left open it will sneak back and crawl again into that empty space. It grew there; it will struggle to stay there. When you discard it, fill up the spot where it was. Replace it with something good. Replace it with unselfish thoughts, with unselfish acts. Then, if an evil habit or addiction tries to return, it will have to fight for attention. . . . You are in charge of you. I repeat, it is very, very difficult to eliminate a bad habit [or sin] just by trying to discard it. Replace it.[11]

In a simple statement to the Thessalonians, the Apostle Paul identified three elements of forsaking sin: (1) turning *from* sin (idolatry); (2) turning *to* God; and (3) living a life of service (see 1 Thessalonians 1:9). Commenting on this passage, one eminent Bible scholar insightfully observed:

No change of mind can be called true repentance without including all three elements. The simple but all too often fact is that true change of mind will necessarily result in change of behavior. Repentance is not merely being ashamed or sorry over sin, although genuine repentance involves an element of remorse. *It is a re-*

*direction of the human will, a purposeful decis[...]
forsake all unrighteousness and pursue righteo[...]
instead. . . .*

Volitionally, repentance involves a *change of direction*, a change of the will. Far from being only a change of mind, it constitutes a willingness—more accurately, a determination—to abandon stubborn disobedience and *surrender the will to Christ.* As such, genuine repentance will inevitably result in a change of behavior.[12]

This "mighty change" of direction and devotion inevitably results in good deeds. John the Baptist referred to these resultant deeds as "fruits worthy of repentance" (see Luke 3:8–14). The book of Jonah indicates that the evidence of the repentance of the people of Nineveh was found in "their works" (see John 3:10). Similarly, Paul taught King Agrippa that to repent meant to "turn to God, and do works meet for repentance" (see Acts 26:20). These good deeds are naturally two-directional—we cannot demonstrate greater love and worship of God without gaining an intensified desire to serve and bless the lives of others. The covenants associated with the ordinance of baptism for the remission of sins require a devotion on our part to *both* God and our fellowmen (see Mosiah 18:8–10). The Book of Mormon clearly teaches this twofold nature of our covenant.

Increased Devotion to God

Alma taught his people at the waters of Mormon that the covenant of baptism involves a commitment or solemn promise to God "that ye will serve him and keep his commandments" (Mosiah 18:10). Writing to his son Moroni, Mormon taught him that "fulfilling the commandments bringeth remission of sins" (Moroni 8:25). In modern times, President Spencer W. Kimball affirmed that "one of the requisites for repentance is the living of the commandments of the Lord. Perhaps few people realize that as an important element; though one may have abandoned a particular sin and even confessed it to his bishop, yet he is not repentant if he has not developed a life of action and service and righteousness, which the Lord has indicated to be very necessary: 'He that repents and does the commandments of the Lord shall be forgiven.' "[13]

The aged prophet Amaleki, prior to transferring custody of the sacred plates to King Benjamin, admonished readers of the Book of Mormon to "come unto Christ, who is the Holy One of Israel, and partake of his salvation, and the power of his redemption. Yea, come unto him, and offer your whole souls as an offering unto him, and *continue in fasting and praying,* and *endure to the end*; and as the Lord liveth ye will be saved [forgiven]." (Omni 1:26; italics added.) Mormon noted this type of transformed lifestyle among the righteous and repentant Nephites in the time of Helaman. "They did fast and pray oft, and did wax stronger and stronger in their humility, and firmer and firmer in the faith of Christ, unto the filling their souls with joy and consolation, yea, even to the purifying and sanctification of their hearts, which sanctification cometh because of their yielding their hearts unto God" (Helaman 3:35). "Yielding" our hearts to God naturally precipitates an increased love for our Heavenly Father and thus increased involvement in his earthly kingdom and more diligent and conscientious efforts to increase our spirituality. Because of the feelings of unworthiness or embarrassment that accompany our sins we may tend to recoil from Church activities and from involvement in spiritual development. Sometimes we may feel unworthy to pray or we may not have a disposition to search the scriptures or fast. Yet these are the very things, institutionally and individually, with which we must now begin to fill our lives. President Spencer W. Kimball wrote:

> Since all of us sin in greater or lesser degree, we are all in need of constant repentance, of continually raising our sights and our performance. One can hardly do the commandments of the Lord in a day, a week, a month or a year. This is an effort which must be extended through the remainder of one's years. To accomplish it every soul should develop the same spirit of devotion and dedication to the work of the Lord as the bishop

and Relief Society president enjoy. Most often theirs is near total devotion.

This devotion needs to be applied as much in mental as in spiritual and physical effort. To understand the gospel so that true obedience can be intelligently given to its requirements takes time and application . . . besides serving and attending and participating in . . . meetings and conferences, and all this in addition to the study of the gospel and many hours on [one's] knees in prayer. . . . Repentance must involve an all-out, total surrender to the program of the Lord.[14]

King Benjamin taught his people that in order for them to *obtain* and *retain* a remission of their sins they must continue in the path of devotion to God. This would include "calling on the name of the Lord daily," "standing steadfastly in the faith," diligently studying the scriptures, and heeding the words of the living prophets in order that we might "grow in the knowledge of the glory of him that created [us]" (see Mosiah 4:11–12). In his discourse, Benjamin clearly pointed out that renewed direction and increased devotion toward God would also have an impact on our devotion toward our fellowmen. "And ye will not have a mind to injure one another," declared King Benjamin, "but to live peaceably, and to render to every man according to that which is his due" (Mosiah 4:13).

Increased Love and Service to Our Fellowmen

Alma taught that if we truly desire to have the heavy burden of sin lifted from our weary shoulders we must be "willing to bear one another's burdens," and to be "willing to mourn with those that mourn; yea, and comfort those that stand in need of comfort" (Mosiah 18:8–9). King Benjamin further declared: "When ye are in the service of your fellow beings ye are only in the service of your God" (Mosiah 2:17). In all the standard works there is perhaps no more profound example of how true repentance engenders a greater desire to serve others than the story of the sons of Mosiah. Before their remarkable conversion these young men were, according to the scriptures, "the very vilest of sinners" (Mosiah 28:4). Because of the sincerity of their repentance and the intensity of their gratitude for the atonement of Christ we later find them "zealously striving to repair all the injuries which they had done to the church, confessing all their sins, and publishing all the things which they had seen, and explaining the prophecies and the scriptures to all who desired to hear them. And thus they were instruments in the hands of God in bringing many to the knowledge of the truth. . . . Now they were desirous that salvation should be declared to every creature." (Mosiah 27:35–36; 28:3.)

Indeed, in several places in the scriptures the Lord indicates a direct relationship between service in the form of missionary work and his ensuing willingness to forgive sins. The Apostle James taught, "Brethren, if any of you do err from the truth, and one convert him; let him know, that he which converteth the sinner from the error of his way shall save a soul from death, and shall hide a multitude of sins" (James 5:19–20). To partake of the blessing of a remission of sins, Alma declared, we must also be willing to "stand as witnesses of God at all times and in all things, and in all places" (Mosiah 18:9). In the current dispensation the Lord has reaffirmed the importance of missionary work and other types of testimony-sharing service in relation to a forgiveness of sins.

> Ye are blessed, for the testimony which ye have borne is recorded in heaven for the angels to look upon; and they rejoice over you, and your sins are forgiven you (D&C 62:3).

> For I will forgive you of your sins *with this commandment* — that you remain steadfast in your minds in solemnity and the spirit of prayer, in bearing testimony to all the world of those things which are communicated unto you (D&C 84:61).

> Whether it be through formal or informal missionary service, work for the dead in the temple, faithfulness in our callings in the Church, or the subtle, simple, often unnoticed service as a home teacher, neighbor, friend, or family member,

we demonstrate our desire to forsake evil by our devotion to others. President Spencer W. Kimball stated:

> A sound way to neutralize the effects of sin in one's life is to bring the light of the gospel to others who do not now enjoy it. This can mean working with both inactive members of the Church and nonmembers. . . .
>
> Every person who is beginning the long journey of emancipating himself from the thralldom of sin and evil will find comfort in the thought expressed by James [James 5:19–20]. We could expand it somewhat and remind the transgressor that every testimony he bears, every prayer he offers, every sermon he preaches, every scripture he reads, every help he gives to stimulate and raise others—all these strengthen him and raise him to higher levels. . . .
>
> Not all of us can engage in full-time missionary work, where one might have opportunity to explain the gospel and bear testimony of its divinity many times every day. . . . But what every member most definitely *can* do is follow President McKay's inspired slogan, "Every member a missionary." . . .
>
> In addition to the possibilities of missionary work, in areas such as quorum and auxiliary and committee work of the Church almost limitless opportunities are afforded to lift others, thus blessing oneself. Monthly there are testimony meetings held where each one has the opportunity to bear witness. To bypass such opportunities is to fail to that extent to pile up credits against the accumulated errors and transgressions.[15]

Restitution

To a large extent this thorough transformation of our lives is a type of restitution or partial repairing of the damaging consequences of our transgressions. However, only the subsequent change of direction and devotion will result in a genuine restitution. There are basically two kinds of restitution—an *immediate*, literal restitution and a *lifelong*, symbolic restitution.

A Literal Restitution

Restitution has always been a significant part of repentance. The literal nature of restitution is delineated in the Old Testament. The law of Moses required a repayment or restoration of that which was stolen or lost through sin. Often this meant paying back even more than was originally lost (see Exodus 22:1–6; Leviticus 6:2–5). In the Church today, we still attempt when possible to "pay back" that which was lost as a result of trespasses. Sometimes it is very easy to make restitution for a sin, when the restitution is something such as paying for or simply returning an item that was stolen. In that case a literal dollar-for-dollar restoration is easy to make. But such restitution is only possible in a few instances. Much more common are deeply damaging consequences for which the path of restitution is not so simple or clear-cut. For some sins only a partial restitution is feasible and in other cases it may actually be impossible to restore that which was lost in any measure. Sometimes all we can do is devote our lives to a lifetime of restitution through righteousness, relying upon the grace of Christ to mercifully rectify that which we could never correct ourselves.

A Lifelong Repayment for Our Sins

By virtue of his infinite and eternal sacrifice the Savior met the demands of justice in our behalf, making it possible for us to be forgiven of our sins and obtain eternal life. When we repent we are no longer subject to the demands of justice but become "indebted" to Christ. He has established repentance, including the mighty change of heart and direction, as the means by which our "indebtedness" is absolved.[16] When we *confess* and *forsake* our sins in the fullest meaning of those words, we make a symbolic payment on our debt to the Savior. By sincere repentance we acknowledge our full faith in him and our total dependence upon his atonement. While it is true that we can in no way, of ourselves, completely repay the Savior, we can show our appreciation for his sacrifice by making symbolic restitution through a lifelong devotion to God and to our fellowmen. Although we will continue to be "unprofitable servants" (Mosiah 2:21), if we truly desire to be forgiven of our sins we will follow the example of the sons of Mosiah, who spent their lives "zealously striving to repair all the injuries" caused by their sins. Few were more faithful and devoted to the Lord and to others than these young men became, "for they could not bear that any human soul should perish" (Mosiah 28:3). Thus, more than mere dollars or transitory deeds is needed to make restitution. Our very lives—our *changed being* as well as our *changed behavior*—verify our awe and appreciation for the atoning blood of Christ that "bought us with a price" and made us "new creatures." Perhaps our lifelong indebtedness—and thus our need for continual restitution—can best be expressed in the poetic words of the thoughtful hymn "Because I Have Been Given Much," written by Grace Noll Crowell.

> Because I have been given much, I too must give;
> Because of thy great bounty, Lord, each day I live
> I shall divide my gifts from thee
> With every brother that I see
> Who has the need of help from me.

> Because I have been sheltered, fed by thy good care,
> I cannot see another's lack and I not share
> My glowing fire, my loaf of bread,
> My roof's safe shelter overhead,
> That he too may be comforted.

> Because I have been blessed by thy great love, dear Lord,
> I'll share thy love again, according to thy word.
> I shall give love to those in need;
> I'll show that love by word and deed:
> Thus shall my thanks be thanks indeed.[17]

(From *Light of the Years,* copyright © 1936 by Harper a͢
Renewed 1964 by Grace Noll Crowell. Used by perr

Notes

1. Spencer W. Kimball, *The Miracle of For*
City: Bookcraft, 1969), p. 203.

2. Joseph F. Smith, *Gospel Doctrine* (Salt Lake City: Deseret Book Co., 1939), p. 100.

3. J. Behm, "Metanoia," in Gerhard Kittel, ed., *Theological Dictionary of the New Testament* (Grand Rapids, Michigan: Eerdmans, 1967), 4:1002.

4. Theodore M. Burton, "The Meaning of Repentance," *Brigham Young University 1984–85 Devotional and Fireside Speeches* (Provo, Utah: Brigham Young University, 1985), p. 97.

5. Spencer W. Kimball, "What Is True Repentance?" *New Era*, May 1974, pp. 4–7.

6. Ibid.

7. Dean L. Larsen, Conference Report, April 1983, p. 48.

8. Ezra Taft Benson, *The Teachings of Ezra Taft Benson* (Salt Lake City: Bookcraft, 1988), p. 71.

9. Orson Pratt, "The Holy Spirit," *A Series of Pamphlets by Orson Pratt* (Liverpool: Franklin D. Richards, 1852), p. 57; republished in *Orson Pratt: Writings of an Apostle* (Salt Lake City: Mormon Heritage Publishers, 1976).

10. Several significant passages throughout the Old Testament use the Hebrew term *shuv* in the context of repentance as "returning to God" rather than just a "turning from sin" (see Genesis 3:19; Leviticus 27:24; Numbers 10:36; Deuteronomy 30:2–8; 1 Samuel 6:3; Isaiah 10:21–22; 19:22; 21:12; 44:22; 51:11; Hosea 2:7–9; 14:1; Malachi 3:7).

11. Boyd K. Packer, *"That All May Be Edified"* (Salt Lake City: Bookcraft, 1982), p. 196.

12. John F. MacArthur, Jr., *The Gospel According to Jesus* (Grand Rapids, Michigan: Zondervan Publishing House, 1988), pp. 162–64; italics added.

13. Spencer W. Kimball, "What Is True Repentance?" *New Era*, May 1974, pp. 4–7.

14. Spencer W. Kimball, *The Miracle of Forgiveness*, pp. 202–3.

15. Ibid., pp. 204–6.

16. For a complete discussion of the role of Christ as our "creditor" and of the way in which our repentance satisfies his conditions for justice and mercy, see Boyd K. Packer, "The Mediator," Conference Report, April 1977, pp. 77–81.

17. Grace Noll Crowell, "Because I Have Been Given Much," *Hymns*, no. 219.

6

"Of You It Is Required to Forgive All Men"

Inherent in a truly reformed and repentant character is a person's willingness to forgive and love those who have trespassed against him. A natural consequence of our newfound sense of gratitude for the "tender mercies of the Lord" (1 Nephi 1:20) should be a heightened desire to extend that same mercy to others. Too often, however, we compartmentalize our repentance, failing to perceive the relationship between *our* change of being and behavior and the feelings we may continue to harbor in our hearts and minds towa others who have offended us. We may erroneously view forgiveness of others as totally independent of or unrel the forgiveness we desire from the Lord. In fact the s make it clear that God's willingness to forgive us i tertwined with our willingness to forgive others our own dispensation, reiterated the divine the Lord, will forgive whom I will forgive, '

quired to forgive all men" (D&C 64:10). This is no arbitrary "do it because I say so" commandment. Like all commandments of God, it is designed to bring about our own individual happiness and ultimate exaltation. The Prophet Joseph Smith declared:

> Whatever God commands is right, no matter what it is, although we may not see the reason thereof till long after the events transpire. . . . But in obedience there is joy and peace unspotted, unalloyed; and as God has designed our happiness—and the happiness of all His creatures, he never has—He never will institute an ordinance or give a commandment to His people that is not calculated in its nature to promote that happiness which He has designed, and which will not end in the greatest amount of good and glory to those who become the recipients of his law and ordinances.[1]

Certainly the commandment to forgive others is designed to promote happiness and good in our lives here on earth and is directly related to the glory that can be ours in the world to come. The Savior taught, by precept and example, the relationship between our forgiving others and the Lord's forgiveness of us. Both types of forgiveness have much to do with our happiness and spiritual development. In the Sermon on the Mount, Jesus taught by precept when he declared: "For if ye forgive men their trespasses, your heavenly Father will also forgive you: but if ye forgive not men their trespasses, neither will your Father forgive your trespasses" (Matthew 6:14–15). He taught this concept by example as well in the Lord's Prayer when he said, "Forgive us our debts, as we forgive our debtors" (Matthew 6:12) and again much later from Golgotha when, incredibly, he pleaded with his Father to "forgive them; for they know not what they do" (Luke 23:34).

On another occasion the Savior illustrated this doctrine through the use of a striking parable. Peter had asked the Master, "How oft shall my brother sin against me, and I forgive him? till seven times?" (Matthew 18:21.) It is evident from Peter's inquiry that he had a limited understanding of he higher law of forgiveness. This deficiency, to a large degree, was due to the Mosaic law's teachings on "eye for an eye" retribution. Peter's follow-up question, "Till seven times?" was intended to be a generous gesture going beyond the requirements of the ancient law. Jesus, however, taught a still higher law when he responded, "I say not unto thee, Until seven times: but, Until seventy times seven" (Matthew 18:22). Certainly the Lord was not saying that we must only forgive four hundred and ninety times, but rather that we must forgive others continually. To further emphasize his point, the Savior then illustrated his higher law of forgiveness with what has become known as the parable of the unmerciful servant.

> Therefore is the kingdom of heaven likened unto a certain king, which would take account of his servants.
>
> And when he had begun to reckon, one was brought unto him, which owed him ten thousand talents.
>
> But forasmuch as he had not to pay, his lord commanded him to be sold, and his wife, and children, and all that he had, and payment to be made.
>
> The servant fell down, and worshipped him, saying, Lord, have patience with me, and I will pay thee all.
>
> Then the lord of that servant was moved with compassion, and loosed him, and forgave him the debt.
>
> But the same servant went out, and found one of his fellowservants, which owed him an hundred pence: and he laid hands on him, and took him by the throat, saying, Pay me that thou owest.
>
> And his fellowservant fell down at his feet, and besought him, saying, Have patience with me, and I will pay thee all.
>
> And he would not: but went and cast him into prison, till he should pay the debt.
>
> So when his fellowservants saw what was done, they were very sorry, and came and told unto their lord all that was done.
>
> Then his lord, after that he had called him, said unto him, O thou wicked servant, I forgave thee all that debt, because thou desiredst me:

Shouldest not thou also have had compassion on thy fellowservant, even as I had pity on thee?

And his lord was wroth, and delivered him to the tormentors, till he should pay all that was due unto him.

So likewise shall my heavenly Father do also unto you, if ye from your hearts forgive not every one his brother their trespasses. (Matthew 18:23–35.)

An understanding of the relative value of this ancient monetary system further illuminates the principle taught in this parable. A talent was equivalent to 60 minas. One mina was equivalent to 100 denarii or pence.[2] This means that the first servant was 600,000 times more indebted to the merciful king than his fellow servant whom he cast into prison for a paltry debt of 100 pence. Just as the first servant was so indebted to the king that he could never repay the debt, so are we "unprofitable servants" in that we are eternally indebted to Christ for his sacrifice on our behalf. This parable dramatically exposes the hypocrisy of petitioning the Lord to forgive our sins, which are ofttimes weighty and grievous, while we withhold forgiveness and mercy from others whose offenses against us may be small or even petty in comparison. Even when the sins against us are more than petty offenses or insignificant indiscretions, even when we have been deeply wounded by heinous crimes or our hearts have been broken by the abominable actions of others, the Lord tells us that if we withhold our forgiveness of others we stand "condemned before the Lord; for there remaineth in [us] the greater sin" (D&C 64:9). We stand "condemned before the Lord" partly because we have chosen by virtue of our unwillingness to forgive others to remain in an unrepentant state. We have not yet experienced the mighty change of heart, and therefore we cannot be forgiven ourselves. In addition, our refusal to forgive others, as reflected in our actions and the intents of our hearts, may be more offensive than the offenses we have suffered. Could it be that "the greater sin" remains with us because our unforgiving spirit reflects a desire on our part to deny or withhold the spiritual healing effects of the Atonement in the lives of others? Is not our stubborn refusal to extend mercy to others a subtle but real rejection of the Redeemer and his redemptive role in the lives of others as well as in our own lives? Such a rejection, whether blatantly acted upon or hypocritically hidden in our hearts, will naturally result in a poisoning of our souls. Feelings of bitterness, hatred, or revenge will retard repentance, stunt our spiritual growth, and place us outside the reach of the Savior's merciful and forgiving arms.

Forgiving Others and the Atonement of Christ

The atonement of Jesus Christ prepared the way, as the prophet Jacob declared, "for our escape from the grasp of this awful monster; yea, that monster, death and hell, which I call the death of the body, and also the death of the spirit" (2 Nephi 9:10). We are the beneficiaries of the Messiah's marvelous mediation. Through his sacrifice we have been unconditionally redeemed from the effects of Adam's fall; through his atoning blood that was spilled in Gethsemane and on Golgotha our lives can be purged of the stains of sin on condition of our repentance. "Wherefore, redemption cometh in and through the Holy Messiah; for he is full of grace and truth," declared father Lehi. "Behold he offereth himself a sacrifice for sin, to answer the ends of the law, unto all those who have a broken heart and a contrite spirit; and unto none else can the ends of the law be answered." (2 Nephi 2:6–7.)

Each of us is dependent upon the Lord Jesus Christ and his mercy to cleanse us from our sins, to work a "mighty change" in our hearts, and to help us develop a celestial character that we may be worthy to return to God's presence. When we repent we are able to "come boldly unto the throne of grace" (Hebrews 4:16) and make claim upon the mercy of the Lord. Yet when we harbor hatred in our hearts and fail to extend our mercy and forgiveness, we would refuse others that same access to "the throne of grace." In essence, we say: "Lord, please forgive me of my sins and extend to me thy mercy and compassion, *but* please don't forgive so-and-so, because he is surely unworthy of thy mercy." Such a selfish and unmerciful attitude is almost Lucifer-like in that we desire to suppress the spiritual development of another and keep him chained in the bonds of sin. Refusing to forgive those who have offended us is assuming the right of judgeship to which we have no claim. Only Jesus has the right to judge others and dispense the prescription of punishment or the medicine of mercy. Elder H. Burke Peterson, while yet a member of the Presiding Bishopric of the Church, eloquently stated:

> Ofttimes *we* choose to decide when a person has repented, and when we will forgive. We have been told mankind will be judged on the intent of the heart. No mortal can see into the depth of another. There is only One who can. His is the role of a judge—not ours. If you are prone to criticize or judge, remember, we never see the target a man aims at in life. We see only what he hits.[3]

Attempting to usurp Christ's right to judge reflects a lack of faith in the justice of God and a reluctance on our part to allow Christ, in his divine role as a perfectly just judge, to "balance the books."

The truth of the matter is that no attempt on our part, whether through our actions or our feelings, can have any impact on the role of the Atonement in the lives of others. Our failure to forgive will not preclude others from partaking of the fruit of the tree of life—which fruit is the love and mercy of Christ. We can only prevent ourselves from tasting of the tree "whose fruit was desirable to make one happy" (1 Nephi 8:10). While we simmer and stew about the sins and souls of others, the effects of *our own sins* remain with us—we cannot be sanctified—and *our own souls* become poisoned with the toxin of bitterness and the venom of vengeance. Bishop H. Burke Peterson illustrated this principle with the following true story:

> Some years ago a group of teenagers from the local high school went on an all-day picnic into the desert on the outskirts of Phoenix. . . . The desert foliage is rather sparse—mostly mesquite, cat-claw, and palo verde trees, with a few cactus scattered here and there. In the heat of the summer, where there are thickets of this

desert growth, you may also find rattlesnakes as unwelcome residents. These young people were picnicking and playing, and during their frolicking, one of the girls was bitten on the ankle by a rattlesnake. As is the case with such a bite, the rattler's fangs released venom almost immediately into her bloodstream.

This very moment was a time of critical decision. They could immediately begin to extract the poison from her leg, or they could search out the snake and destroy it. Their decision made, the girl and her young friends pursued the snake. It slipped quickly into the undergrowth and avoided them for fifteen or twenty minutes. Finally, they found it, and rocks and stones soon avenged the infliction.

Then they remembered: their companion had been bitten! They became aware of her discomfort, as by now the venom had had time to move from the surface of the skin deep into the tissues of her foot and leg. Within another thirty minutes they were at the emergency room of the hospital. By then, the venom was well into its work of destruction.

A couple of days later I was informed of the incident and was asked by some young members of the Church to visit their friend in the hospital. As I entered her room, I saw a pathetic sight. Her foot and leg were elevated—swollen almost beyond recognition. The tissue in her limb had been destroyed by the poison, and a few days later it was found her leg would have to be amputated below the knee.

It was a senseless sacrifice, this price of revenge. How much better it would have been if, after the young woman had been bitten, there had been an extraction of the venom from the leg in a process known to all desert dwellers.[4]

All too often we become "victims," like this snake-bitten young lady. The most painful wounds to our minds, hearts, and souls are usually self-inflicted. As victims of self-inflicted suffering, we become tormented not so much by the offenses against us as by our own unforgiving thoughts and attitudes.

Because we would withhold the forgiving effects of the Atonement from others, we are the ones left unforgiven. This suffering is, as Elder Boyd K. Packer stated, "unnecessary suffering," but if we do not get rid of the burdensome feelings in our hearts our "self-inflicted penalties soon become cruel and unusual punishment."[5] Hence we stand "condemned before the Lord"—with soul cankered from a cruel and unusual punishment we execute upon ourselves.

An Unwillingness to Forgive Cankers the Soul

All too often we fall into the unfortunate condition of condemning the unforgiving hearts around us while failing to recognize those same symptoms in ourselves. "We are all prone to brood on the evil done us," President Gordon B. Hinckley stated. "That brooding becomes as a gnawing and destructive canker. . . . There is no peace in the nursing of a grudge. There is no happiness in living for the day when you can 'get even.' "[6] An example from literature poignantly portrays how such brooding and bitterness can actually serve to destroy one's own soul. The French writer Guy de Maupassant wrote of a peasant man named Hauchecome who had come to the village on market day to buy some goods.

> While walking through the public square, his eye caught sight of a piece of string lying on the cobblestones. He picked it up and put it in his pocket. His actions were observed by the village harness maker with whom he had previously had a dispute.
>
> Later in the day the loss of a purse was reported. Hauchecome was arrested on the accusation of the harness maker. He was taken before the mayor, to whom he protested his innocence, showing the piece of string that he had picked up. But he was not believed and was laughed at.
>
> The next day the purse was found, and Hauchecome was absolved of any wrongdoing. But, resentful of the indignity he had suffered because of a false accusation, he became embittered and would not let the

matter die. Unwilling to forgive and forget, he thought and talked of little else. He neglected his farm. Everywhere he went, everyone he met had to be told of the injustice. By day and by night he brooded over it. Obsessed with his grievance, he became desperately ill and died. In the delirium of his death struggles, he repeatedly murmured, "A piece of string, a piece of string."[7]

The sad demise of Hauchecome may be only a fictional account, but it certainly could represent the very real spiritual decline of many people. Each of us knows of acquaintances, friends, or family members who have slowly destroyed themselves spiritually and emotionally by harboring bitterness and resentment. These examples often attest to the truthfulness of the adage, "For the man with no forgiveness in his heart, life is worse than death."

While many who are unforgiving may not suffer this total self-destruction, their spiritual progress still becomes stymied to one degree or another. It may start as a simple grudge, but gradually and almost imperceptibly it can cause a serious shrinkage of our souls. Some thoughtful person once said, "Forgiving makes us free for giving." The opposite is also true. *When we fail to forgive, we fail to give.* It becomes increasingly more difficult for us to reach beyond ourselves because we become more self-centered and more focused on our own hurts rather than on healing the hurts of others. This in turn prevents us from obtaining the joy, blessings, and spiritual growth that come only from service. Thus we find ourselves in a vicious downward cycle which we can only break by freeing ourselves from the ties of bitterness that bind us ever tighter.

"In Your Hearts": Forgiveness and the Laws of Justice

The Lord declared to the Prophet Joseph Smith:

My disciples, in days of old, sought occasion against one another and forgave not one another *in their hearts,* and *for this evil they were afflicted and sorely chastened.*

Wherefore, I say unto you, that ye ought to forgive one another; for he that forgiveth not his brother his trespasses standeth condemned before the Lord; for there remaineth in him the greater sin.

I, the Lord, will forgive whom I will forgive, but of you it is required to forgive all men.

And ye ought to say *in your hearts*—let God judge between me and thee, and reward thee according to thy deeds. (D&C 64:8–11; italics added.)

Perhaps the most important words in the foregoing revelation are the oft-overlooked phrases "in their hearts" and "in your hearts." True forgiveness emanates from the heart. When our hearts are not cleansed and purified of all ill will, no outward gesture of reconciliation will have any meaning. On the other hand, if our hearts are free from bitterness and the desire for revenge we may actually take actions that appear on the surface to indicate a lack of forgiveness, when in reality we are only allowing justice to be served. These concepts can be illustrated by the following examples.

Several years ago, someone had trespassed against a member of my family and had thus offended me in turn. I held a grudge and found myself soon disliking the offender immensely. Recognizing that I was harboring ill feelings, I made halfhearted efforts to do things that could be perceived as forgiveness. I gave the person things that were important to me. I spoke to the person at church and made conscious efforts to be friendly. I soon discovered that instead of feeling better, I was feeling worse. The cankering of my soul continued. Even though I was making token gestures of forgiveness I was not yet willing to forgive *in my heart.* Until my heart was right and I was willing to "let go" of my feelings of bitterness, my pretensions of forgiveness brought no lasting peace to my soul.

A second example illustrates the other end of this continuum. A student shared with me the following true story:

Several years ago my brother asked if we would take into our home his son. The son was having some problems and it was thought that it might help straighten him out to live with some family other than his own. We agreed to the arrangement and did all we could to make him feel welcome and a part of our family. I provided him with a job and expected him to work just like all the other employees. It wasn't long until we . . . discovered money missing from our house and from the business. We suspected our nephew of stealing the money, but tried to be patient and work with him in hopes that we could help straighten him out. It wasn't long until one of the company pickups came up missing and we soon discovered that our nephew had stolen it and had driven back to his hometown to "party" with his old friends.

After a few weeks he came back to us and said he was sorry for what he had done and told us that he wanted another chance to straighten up and to make it up to us. We forgave him and let him once again stay in our home and work for us. Things went pretty well for a while, but one day when we came home from work we found our home ransacked and burglarized. Many of our valuables had been taken and we soon discovered that several thousand dollars and a truck from our business had also been stolen. Almost immediately we knew that our nephew was again the culprit. We agonized over what we should do. We knew that if we got the police involved we might alienate my brother and his family against us. Should we just forgive and forget?

We finally decided to call the police and press charges against our nephew. Today he is in prison as a result of the crimes he perpetrated against us. We have felt guilty for all this time for prosecuting him. We have been left to wonder if we did the right thing. Should we have just turned the other cheek? How can we forgive him yet protect ourselves? How can we forgive and forget when we have been so deeply hurt? Did we do the wrong thing? We have so many questions that I wonder if we really know what forgiveness is.

Both of these cases illustrate a degree of confusion as to what constitutes forgiveness of others. In each instance there was an overemphasis on what one *does* almost to the exclusion of what one *feels*. The feelings "in your hearts," as stressed by the Lord in the revelations, are a more reliable barometer of true forgiveness. It may be that this confusion is created to a degree by a tendency to focus too much on sensational stories of almost superhuman acts of forgiveness. We have become familiar with stories of remarkable people like the family who not only forgave the delinquent young man who killed their son in a traffic accident but took him into their own home as a foster child. Another is the story in Church curriculum materials of Chief Sam Blue of the Catawba Indian tribe who, through determined faith and prayer, was able to forgive and shake hands with the men who had deliberately, in the guise of a hunting "accident," killed his son.

These stories may inspire some people, but they may actually discourage others. If we compare ourselves only to these "superhuman forgivers," we may come to feel that we are being forgiving only if we are able to perform some magnanimous gesture toward our offender. Speaking of forgiving others who have done us grievous wrong, President Gordon B. Hinckley observed: "Most of us have not reached that stage of compassion and love and forgiveness. It is not easy. It requires a self-discipline almost greater than we are capable of."[8] Thus, overcoming acrimonious, vengeful feelings *in our hearts* is sometimes a monumental accomplishment in itself. Generous acts of charity may follow as we replace hate with love, but they are not necessarily required by the Lord.

When we seek to hold ourselves to a preconceived standard of forgiveness which is above and beyond what the Lord has revealed in the scriptures, we may become discouraged and may inflict unnecessary emotional and spiritual pain upon ourselves. This is evident in the almost despondent pleading of one woman who searchingly asked: "How can I ever truly forgive my ex-husband, who physically and sexually abused our children, when I refuse to allow him in our home or near our children?" She was confusing the *action* of accepting her ex-husband back into their home (which might actually be unwise or even hazardous to the welfare of the family) with the *feeling* of forgiveness that must prevail "in your hearts." She did not realize that she could still forgive in her heart and yet wisely protect herself and her family from further injury. Likewise, we must not confuse forgiveness of others with the right to allow the laws of justice, both legal and spiritual, to operate in their lives. In his classic work *Mere Christianity* C. S. Lewis differentiated between loving your enemy and punishing him. His words could apply equally well to forgiving others.

> Does loving your enemy mean not punishing him? No, for loving myself does not mean that I ought not to subject myself to punishment—even to death. If one had committed a murder, the right Christian thing to do would be to give yourself up to the police and be hanged. It is therefore, in my opinion, perfectly right for a Christian judge to sentence a man to death. . . .
>
> I imagine somebody will say, "well, if one is allowed to condemn the enemy's acts, and punish him, and kill him, what difference is left between Christian morality and the ordinary view?" All the difference in the world. . . . What really matters is those little marks or twists on the central, inside part of the soul which are going to turn it, in the long run, into a heavenly or hellish creature. . . . *We may punish if necessary, but we must not enjoy it. In other words, something inside us, the feeling of resentment, the feeling that wants to get one's own back, must be simply killed.*[9]

Perhaps no event in the history of this latter-day Church better exemplifies the need for forgiveness versus the demands for justice than the suffering of the Saints in Missouri during the period of extreme persecution and barbaric treatment brought about by Governor Boggs's infamous "extermination order." Did the Lord's commandment to "forgive all men" apply to the Mormons who were being driven cruelly and unlawfully from their homes? Were the Saints required to forgive these ruthless ruffians who had committed assault, murder, rape, and robbery? To both questions the answer is a resounding yes. None of us, regardless of the depth or breadth of our injuries, is exempt from the commandment to "forgive all men."

The Prophet Joseph reaffirmed this to the suffering Saints in Missouri by encouraging them to forgive "in their hearts" and not to seek retaliation or revenge. Yet he further counselled them: "We must be wise as serpents and harmless as doves. . . . It is your privilege to use every lawful means in your power to seek redress for your grievances from your enemies, and prosecute them to the extent of the law."[10] In our day a modern Apostle, Elder Boyd K. Packer, reemphasized the principle. "There is no dishonor," he declared, "in appealing to a court of law for either justice or protection."[11] Even though there is no dishonor in exercising our legal rights for protection and justice, we must ensure that our motives are pure and that the spirit of forgiveness has replaced any resentment and desire for retaliation. It is for this reason that the Lord's all-seeing eye will focus more on our hearts than just on our outward actions. In this vein, C. S. Lewis observed:

> We believe that God forgives us our sins; but also that He will not do so unless we forgive other people their sins against us. There is no doubt about the second part of this statement. It is in the Lord's Prayer; it was emphatically stated by our Lord. If you don't forgive you will not be forgiven. No part of His teaching is clearer, *and there are no exceptions to it.* He doesn't say that we are to forgive other people's sins provided they are not too frightful, or provided there are extenuating circumstances, or anything of that sort. *We are to forgive them all, however spiteful, however mean, however often they are repeated. If we don't we shall be forgiven none of our own.* . . . Forgiving does not mean excusing. Many people seem to think that it does. They think that if you ask them to forgive someone who has cheated or bullied them you are trying to make out that

there was really no cheating or bullying. But if that were so there would be nothing to forgive. They keep on replying, "But I tell you the man broke a solemn promise." Exactly: that is precisely what you have to forgive. *(This doesn't mean that you must necessarily believe his next promise. It does mean that you must make every effort to kill every taste of resentment in your own heart—every wish to humiliate or hurt him or to pay him out.)*

. . . We are offered forgiveness on no other terms. *To refuse it is to refuse God's mercy for ourselves.* There is no hint of exceptions and God means what he says.[12]

A Heart-Healing and Soul-Soothing Application of the Balm of Gilead

For virtually every Latter-day Saint who desires to do what is right, the question is not "Should I forgive those who have offended or harmed me in any manner?" but rather "How can I forgive them?" Even when we have experienced marvelous spiritual manifestations in our lives, even when we feel that we possess unshakable testimonies of the truthfulness of the gospel, even with a seemingly sure foundation of spiritual strength—even then, our ability to forgive others may be our most difficult and demanding test of true discipleship. William Jennings Bryan, the eloquent American statesman, observed: "The most difficult of all the virtues to cultivate is the forgiving spirit."[13] Man's natural inclination is to fight back when wronged or hurt. But although it may be "natural" to seek revenge, the ancient words of King Benjamin serve as a restraining reminder:

> For the natural man is an enemy to God, and has been from the fall of Adam, and will be, forever and ever, unless he yields to the enticings of the Holy Spirit, and *putteth off the natural man and becometh a Saint through the atonement of Christ the Lord* (Mosiah 3:19; italics added).

At times it may seem not only difficult but virtually impossible to overcome our natural inclinations toward resentment and retribution. Yet even if we think it impossible, the Lord assures us that forgiveness is not only possible but also required (see D&C 64:7–12). On this point President Spencer W. Kimball declared:

> Hard to do? Of course. The Lord never promised an easy road, nor a simple gospel, nor low standards, nor a low norm. The price is high, but the goods attained are worth all they cost. The Lord himself turned the other cheek; he suffered himself to be buffeted and beaten without remonstrance; he suffered every indignity and yet spoke no word of condemnation. And his question to all of us is: "Therefore, what manner of man ought ye to be?" And his answer to us is: "Even as I am." (3 Ne. 27:27.) . . .
>
> It can be done. Man can conquer self. Man can overcome. Man can forgive all who have trespassed against him and go on to receive *peace* in this life and eternal life in the world to come.[14]

Several years ago after I had given a lecture on the subject of forgiving others a woman approached me with a crucial question: "What can I do to rid myself of the terrible feelings and hatred that I have in my heart for someone who deeply hurt and betrayed me?" I tried as well as I could to explain what the scriptures taught, but she was not satisfied with my answer. She seemed to be seeking some "quick-fix, self-help program" for forgiving others. She had, as she explained, "tried so many things," but the hatred in her heart remained. The longer we talked, the more I realized that she had not understood that it was *impossible* for her to forgive and cleanse her heart of bitterness *all by herself*. She failed to see that we overcome the "natural man" not only by our own efforts to "forgive and forget" but also, and more important, "through the atonement of Christ the Lord."

The beauty of this principle is illustrated symbolically by the balm of Gilead referred to in the Old Testament. In ancient times a major export to Tyre and Egypt was an ointment made from the aromatic gum of resin-producing bushes surrounding Gilead. This balm of Gilead was renowned throughout the ancient Near East for its soothing and healing properties. Even today the phrase *balm of Gilead* symbolizes a spiritual power that can soothe the soul and heal the heart.

> There is a Balm in Gilead,
> To make the wounded whole,
> There is a Balm in Gilead,
> To heal the sin-sick soul.[15]

Both symbolically and literally, the afflicted person must make a generous application of the ointment to his own wounds in order to experience the miraculous healing promised. While each of us must do certain things to "apply" the balm of Gilead, the actual healing of the heart comes *only* from the Lord.

A gripping story from the life of Corrie ten Boom beautifully illustrates this twofold nature of forgiving others. Corrie ten Boom, a Christian woman living in Holland, was arrested by the Nazi Gestapo for hiding Dutch Jews during World War II. She was sent to a concentration camp, and her remarkable story of faith and survival in the death camps is told in her book *The Hiding Place.* Years after the war and her liberation from the concentration camps she went to Germany to speak to congregations and to testify of the loving and forgiving nature of God. It was at one of these meetings where her Christian character and professed belief in forgiveness were ultimately tested.

> It was in a church in Munich that I saw him—a balding, heavyset man in a gray overcoat, a brown felt hat clutched between his hands. People were filing out of the basement room where I had just spoken, moving along the rows of wooden chairs to the door at the rear. It was 1947 and I had come from Holland to defeated Germany with the message that God forgives.
>
> It was the truth they needed most to hear in that bitter, bombed-out land, and I gave them my favorite mental picture. Maybe because the sea is not far from a Hollander's mind, I liked to think that that's where forgiven sins were thrown. "When we confess our sins," I

said, "God casts them into the deepest ocean, gone forever. . . ."

The solemn faces stared back at me, not quite daring to believe. There were never questions after a talk in Germany in 1947. People stood up in silence, in silence collected their wraps, in silence left the room.

And that's when I saw him, working his way forward against the others. One moment I saw the overcoat and the brown hat; the next, a blue uniform and a visored cap with its skull and crossbones. It came back with a rush: the huge room with its harsh overhead lights; the pathetic pile of dresses and shoes in the center of the floor; the shame of walking naked past this man. I could see my frail sister's form ahead of me, ribs sharp beneath the parchment skin. *Betsie, how thin you were!*

[Betsie and I had been arrested for concealing Jews in our home during the Nazi occupation of Holland; this man had been a guard at Ravensbruck concentration camp where we were sent.]

Now he was in front of me, hand thrust out: "A fine message, Fräulein! How good it is to know that, as you say, all our sins are at the bottom of the sea."

And I, who had spoken so glibly of forgiveness, fumbled in my pocketbook rather than take that hand. He would not remember me, of course—how could he remember one prisoner among those thousands of women?

But I remembered him and the leather crop swinging from his belt. I was face to face with one of my captors and my blood seemed to freeze.

"You mentioned Ravensbruck in your talk," he was saying. "I was a guard there." No, he did not remember me.

"But since that time," he went on, "I have become a Christian. I know that God has forgiven me for the cruel things I did there, but I would like to hear it from your lips as well. Fräulein,"—again the hand came out —"will you forgive me?"

And I stood there—I whose sins had again and

again to be forgiven—and could not forgive. Betsie had died in that place—could he erase her slow terrible death simply for the asking?

It could not have been many seconds he stood there —hand held out—but to me it seemed hours as I wrestled with the most difficult thing I had ever had to do.

For I had to do it—I knew that. The message that God forgives has a prior condition: that we forgive those who have injured us. "If you do not forgive men their trespasses," Jesus says, "neither will your Father in heaven forgive your trespasses."

I knew it not only as a commandment of God, but as a daily experience. Since the end of the war I had had a home in Holland for victims of Nazi brutality. Those who were able to forgive their former enemies were able to return to the outside world and rebuild their lives, no matter what the physical scars. Those who nursed their bitterness remained invalids. It was as simple and as horrible as that.

And I still stood there with coldness clutching my heart. But forgiveness is not an emotion—I knew that too. Forgiveness is an act of the will, and the will can function regardless of the temperature of the heart. "Jesus, help!" I prayed silently. "I can lift my hand. I can do that much. You supply the feeling."

And so woodenly, mechanically, I thrust my hand into the one stretched out to me. And as I did, an incredible thing took place. The current started in my shoulder, raced down my arm, sprang into our joined hands. And then this healing warmth seemed to flood my whole being, bringing tears to my eyes.

"I forgive you, brother!" I cried. "With all my heart!"

For a long moment we grasped each other's hands, the former guard and the former prisoner. I had never known God's love so intensely as I did then.[16]

Just as Corrie ten Boom was able to experience the God-given warmth of forgiveness *only after* she supplied the forgiving handshake, we too must be willing to perform certain volitional acts of forgiveness in order for God to "supply the feeling." There are at least three fundamental things we can do so that God can endow us with this spirit of forgiveness, love, and peace.

"Leave It Alone"

The Chinese philosopher Confucius declared: "To be wronged or robbed is nothing unless you continue to remember it."[17] All too often we cling tenaciously to our grievances against those who have wronged us—mulling them over and over in our minds. Until we are willing to "let go" of our spiteful thoughts and emotions, we remain bound by our own self-imposed bonds of bitterness. We become like some small animals, such as monkeys or raccoons, that are easily trapped by a simple box with a hole in it just large enough for the animal to reach in and retrieve a morsel of food or a curious object. The hole, however, is too small to allow a fist formed by clinging to the object to come out again. The animal, unwilling to let go of the bait, is thus trapped.

The ideal attitude, "forgive and forget," may seem unrealistic, if not impossible to achieve. Each of us will cognitively remember how we have been wronged or injured, but we can indeed "forget" in the sense that we can conscientiously commit or covenant to "let go" of our hard feelings. We can determine to dwell no longer on the wrongs done us. We can force thoughts of retribution out of our minds. Elder Boyd K. Packer counseled:

> I say therefore, "John, leave it alone. Mary, leave it alone." . . .
>
> Some frustrations we must endure without really solving the problem. Some things that ought to be put in order are not put in order because we cannot control them. Things we cannot solve, we must survive.
>
> If you resent someone for something he has done—or failed to do—forget it.
>
> Too often the things we carry are petty, even stu-

pid. If you are still upset after all these years because Aunt Clara didn't come to your wedding reception, why don't you grow up and forget it?

If you brood constantly over a loss or a past mistake, look ahead—settle it.

We call that forgiveness. Forgiveness is powerful spiritual medicine.[18]

This "leaving alone" of deeds that are done and cannot be undone and of circumstances that are beyond our control is the first step in preparing our hearts for the healing that God alone can bestow.

"Do Good to Them That Hate You"

The Savior taught an even higher ideal when he explained that we must extend mercy and kindness to those that have harmed us.

Ye have heard that it hath been said, Thou shalt love thy neighbour, and hate thine enemy.

But I say unto you, *Love* your enemies, *bless* them that curse you, *do good* to them that hate you, and *pray* for them which despitefully use you, and persecute you. (Matthew 5:43–44; italics added.)

Often the question arises, "How can I love my enemies or those who have hurt me when I have no feelings of affection for them or when I actually dislike them?" The Savior's celestial charge is based not on emotion but on volition. The phrases he used—"love," "bless," "pray"—imply *actions we choose to do* rather than feelings that we naturally feel. Just as "letting go" involves a conscientious commitment on our part, so does this second prescript. Dr. M. Scott Peck, noted psychiatrist and author of the best-seller *The Road Less Traveled*, made this observation about loving others:

It is possible to love . . . without loving feelings, and it is in the fulfillment of this possibility that genuine and transcendent love is distinguished from simple [affection]. The key word in this distinction is "will." I have defined love as the *will* to extend oneself for the purpose of nurturing one's own or another's spiritual

growth. Genuine love is volitional rather than emotional. The person who truly loves does so because of a
decision to love. This person has made a commitment
to be loving whether or not the loving feeling is present.[19]

As mentioned, there need not necessarily be any magnanimous gesture. However, there can be simple sentiments of
spiritual concern and Christlike compassion like those at-
tained by the sons of Mosiah who "could not bear that any
human soul should perish" (Mosiah 28:3). Loving our enemies may not involve liking them or their deeds, but it must
involve a commitment to "clothe [ourselves] with the bond
of charity" (D&C 88:125) that extends to all our brothers and
sisters. C. S. Lewis elucidated on loving our enemies and
doing good to those that hate us.

> The rule for all of us is perfectly simple. Do not waste
> time bothering whether you "love" your neighbour; act
> as if you did. As soon as we do this we find one of the
> great secrets. When you are behaving as if you loved
> someone, you will presently come to love him. . . . If
> you do him a good turn, you will find yourself disliking
> him less. . . . The difference between a Christian and a
> worldly man is not that the worldly man has only affec-
> tions or "likings" and the Christian has only "charity."
> The worldly man treats certain people kindly because
> he "likes" them: the Christian, trying to treat every one
> kindly, finds himself liking more and more people as he
> goes on—including people he could not have even ima-
> gined himself liking in the beginning.
>
> We must try to feel about the enemy as we feel
> about ourselves—to wish that he were not bad, to
> hope that he may, in this world or another, be cured: in
> fact, to wish his good. That is what is meant in the
> Bible by loving him: *wishing his good*, not feeling fond
> of him nor saying he is nice when he is not.[20]

The more we extend our compassion and charity to our
enemies by ". . . pray[ing] for them which despitefully use
[us], and persecute [us]" (Matthew 5:44), the more our icy

feelings of hatred or resentment are melted away. When we are unselfishly and compassionately praying for our enemies, we can in turn come confidently before our Father and petition in our own behalf.

"Pray unto the Father with All the Energy of Heart"

Mormon, speaking of such charity—the pure love of Christ —wrote: "Pray unto the Father with all the energy of heart, that ye may be filled with this love" (Moroni 7:48). Likewise, as we let go of all bitterness and put pettiness behind us, as we do good to and pray for those who have injured us, we must also plead with our Heavenly Father to fill our hearts with the true spirit of forgiveness. President Gordon B. Hinckley has prophetically promised that such pleadings will not go unanswered.

> If there be any within the sound of my voice who nurture in their hearts the poisonous brew of enmity toward another, I plead with you to ask the Lord for strength to forgive. This expression of desire will be of the very substance of your repentance. It may not be easy, and it may not come quickly. But if you will seek it with sincerity and cultivate it, it *will* come. . . . There will come into your heart a peace otherwise unattainable.[21]

As President Hinckley emphasized, this promised peace and change of heart may not come quickly nor easily. We must remember, however, that the promise is sure even though its attainment may be gradual. The following true story demonstrates the fulfillment of the promise that God will indeed "supply the feeling" when we "supply the actions."

> [One of the challenges of my life] was an individual I had to work closely with. I felt no particular admiration for him and he obviously held me in great disdain. As our interchanges grew more prickly, I found him deliberately trying to sabotage my work and needling me to provoke quarrels. I responded in the best tradition of

the natural man and soon a bitter feud was under way. In my quieter moments, I realized that I was destroying myself and that the Spirit was leaving me because of this contention.

Again, I turned to the Lord and prayed, night and morning, "Father, I'm having a terrible time with this man. Wilt thou bless me that I may feel about him as thou dost." Soon a vision began to open to me of an entirely different person than the one I'd been perceiving. I now saw a sensitive, easily hurt individual who felt alone, vulnerable, and afraid in new situations. I began to see the great strengths he had developed. . . . I gradually came to feel reverence and even awe for him. Here was a son of God, beloved and cherished of him. And who could resist loving such a person? Not I. It came. *The love just came.* Another small corner of my heart had been changed, and the Lord's promise had been fulfilled.[22]

Notes

1. Joseph Smith, *Teachings of the Prophet Joseph Smith,* compiled by Joseph Fielding Smith (Salt Lake City: Deseret Book Co., 1938), pp. 256–57.

2. *Eerdman's Handbook to the Bible,* edited by David and Pat Alexander (Grand Rapids, Michigan: Eerdmans Publishing Co., 1973), pp. 108–9. (See also LDS Bible Dictionary, pp. 733–34.)

3. H. Burke Peterson, Conference Report, October 1983, p. 85.

4. Ibid., pp. 83–84.

5. Boyd K. Packer, "Balm of Gilead," *Ensign,* November 1987, p. 16.

6. Gordon B. Hinckley, Conference Report, October 1980, p. 87.

7. Ibid., p. 86. (See also *The Works of Guy de Maupassant* [Black's Reader Service: Roslyn, New York], pp. 34–38.)

8. Gordon B. Hinckley, "The Healing Power of Christ," *Ensign*, November 1988, p. 59.

9. C. S. Lewis, *Mere Christianity* (London: Collins Fount, 1960), pp. 106–7; italics added.

10. Joseph Smith, *History of the Church*, 1:448–51, 453–56.

11. Boyd K. Packer, "Balm of Gilead," *Ensign*, November 1987, p. 16.

12. C. S. Lewis, "On Forgiveness," *The Weight of Glory* (New York: Macmillan Publishing Co., 1949), pp. 121–22, 124–25; italics added.

13. William Jennings Bryan, *The Prince of Peace* (Independence, Missouri: Zion's Printing and Publishing Co., 1925), p. 35.

14. Spencer W. Kimball, Conference Report, October 1977, pp. 71–72.

15. *Recreational Songs* (Salt Lake City: The Church of Jesus Christ of Latter-day Saints, 1949), p. 130; as quoted by Elder Boyd K. Packer in "Balm of Gilead," *Ensign*, November 1987, p. 16.

16. From Corrie ten Boom, "I'm Still Learning to Forgive," *Guideposts*, November 1972.

17. Confucius, as quoted by Spencer W. Kimball, Conference Report, October 1977, p. 72.

18. Boyd K. Packer, "Balm of Gilead," *Ensign*, November 1987, p. 18.

19. M. Scott Peck, *The Road Less Traveled* (New York: Touchstone, 1978), p. 119.

20. C. S. Lewis, *Mere Christianity*, pp. 116–17, 108.

21. Gordon B. Hinckley, Conference Report, October 1980, p. 87.

22. Dennis R. Peterson, "To Love the Things God Loves," *Ensign*, March 1981, p. 7.

7

Knowing You Are Forgiven

Seated across the desk from me was a young woman with a heavy heart, a young woman whose eyes seemed to plead for an answer to the important doctrinal question she posed to me. "How will I know when the Lord has forgiven me? I have tried with all my heart to repent and make amends, but nothing has happened in my life to tell me that I am forgiven." She continued, "Is there something else I must do? What does it feel like to obtain a remission of sins?"

Her situation was unique and personal to her, but the questions were not unique. Thousands of people have either silently pondered or verbally posed those same questions. There is, however, no prescribed set of answers that will explicitly and completely describe all of the conditions and/or feelings that for every person will accompany a remission of sins. Trying to answer the question "How will I know when I am forgiven?" is somewhat like trying to respond to the query "How do you know when you have the companionship of the Holy Ghost?" or "How do you know you possess a testimony?" One simple statement, explanation, or definition would be insufficient, and such a statement certainly could not be applied to every individual. Different people often experience the same spiritual event in different ways. However there are also many shared feelings and experiences associated with testimony or spirituality. So it is with knowing we have been forgiven. Each of us may come to know in different ways and under different circumstances, but the scriptures and latter-day prophets attest to the reality of the Lord's promise of forgiveness and illuminate some of the "indicators" that accompany this great cleansing experience.

One of the indicators, spoken of previously, is the change that is wrought within us by the Holy Ghost. "The actual cleansing of the soul," wrote Elder Bruce R. McConkie, "comes when the Holy Ghost is received. The Holy Ghost is a sanctifier whose divine commission is to burn dross and evil out of a human soul as though by fire."[1] The Savior referred to it as being "born again," being "born of the Spirit" (see John 3:7–8), and as a "baptism with fire" (see 3 Nephi 9:20). Alma called this experience "a mighty change in your hearts" (see Alma 5:14), and Paul spoke of it as becoming "a new creature" in Christ (see 2 Corinthians 5:17). Each of these terms, including "conversion" and "spiritual rebirth," refer to the spiritual transformation from evil to good that comes to us by virtue of the atonement of Jesus Christ upon condition of our faith and repentance. Because of its deeply spiritual nature, the "baptism with fire" and the remission of sins that accompanies it cannot be precisely described nor defined for all people. There are parallels for this situation. For example, a person without formal training in principles of science may not fully understand the technical definition of fire, but he can see what it does and know how it feels. Similarly, we may not fully *understand* how our sins are remitted, but when we *experience* this "spiritual rebirth" we will *feel* and *know* that the Lord has forgiven our sins.

Some Spiritual Indicators of the "Baptism of Fire"

The words and lives of Enos, Alma, King Benjamin, the Apostle Paul, and others provide us with valuable insights into what one *feels* and *does* when he is cleansed by the atonement of Christ. The following scriptural examples of spiritual rebirth are not intended to be an exhaustive, all-inclusive checklist of experiences we must have in order to consider ourselves forgiven; rather, they serve as inspiring examples and illustrative guides for knowing when we are forgiven and to what extent we have been "born again."

Peace of Conscience

Enos told of an experience which lasted all day and into the night and which he referred to as a "wrestle" with God in "mighty prayer and supplication." As he cried unto the Lord the desire of his heart was granted when the Lord spoke to him and said, "Enos, thy sins are forgiven thee, and thou shalt be blessed" (Enos 1:5). One of the most significant indicators of a remission of sins is found in Enos' declaration, "My guilt was swept away" (Enos 1:6). Approximately four centuries after Enos, King Benjamin's people experienced a similar feeling after their prayer of penitence: "O have mercy, and apply the atoning blood of Christ that we may receive forgiveness of our sins, and our hearts may be purified" (Mosiah 4:2). The scriptural record recounts the miraculous spiritual rebirth which effected a remission of their sins and was accompanied by a "peace of conscience, because of the exceeding faith which they had in Jesus Christ" (Mosiah 4:3). Like Enos, King Benjamin's people experienced a sweet spiritual feeling that "swept away" guilty feelings and replaced them with a "peace of conscience" that quietly yet profoundly testified that the people's sins were "remember[ed] no more" (see D&C 58:42). President Harold B. Lee, commenting on this passage and its application to all who have struggled to know if the Lord has forgiven them, said:

Some years ago, President Romney and I were sitting in my office. The door opened and a fine young man came in with a troubled look on his face, and he said, "Brethren, I am going to the temple for the first time tomorrow. I have made some mistakes in the past, and I have gone to my bishop and my stake president, and I have made a clean disclosure of it all; and after a period of repentance and assurance that I have not returned again to those mistakes, they have now adjudged me ready to go to the temple. But, brethren, that is not enough. I want to know, and how can I know, that the Lord has forgiven me, also."

What would you answer one who would come to you asking that question? As we pondered for a moment, we remembered King Benjamin's address contained in the book of Mosiah. . . .

If the time comes when you have done all that you can to repent of your sins, whoever you are, wherever you are, and have made amends and restitution to the best of your ability; if it be something that will affect your standing in the Church and you have gone to the proper authorities, then you will want that confirming answer as to whether or not the Lord has accepted of you. In your soul-searching, if you seek for and you find that *peace of conscience*, by that token you may know that the Lord has accepted of your repentance.[2]

Unfortunately, some people have mistakenly felt that their sins were not forgiven as long as they continued to remember them. Alma's counsel to his sons, which included a recounting of his own dramatic conversion and the consequent remission of his sins, dispels this misconception and teaches the proper relationship between peace of conscience and the remembrance of sins. It is obvious from Alma's record that he could vividly remember his sins nearly a generation later. He could remember not only what sins he had committed but also the consequences of his actions and the exquisite spiritual pain that resulted. To his sons he described his relief upon receiving a remission of his sins: "I could remember my pains no more; I was harrowed up by the memory of my sins

no more'' (Alma 36:19). Although he could continue to remember his sins and even the pain that he had suffered, his
conscience was no longer tortured by guilt. Each of us, like
Alma, may continue to remember our sins and, to a degree,
the feelings of remorse associated with them. Our Father in
Heaven desires that we should remember so that we may not
so easily fall prey again to the wiles of the devil. It is for our
instruction and benefit that the Lord allows us to retain a remembrance of our sins; but through repentance the ''harrow-
ing'' or debilitating effects of a guilt-ridden conscience are
removed and instead comes a peace of conscience that might
cause us to declare, as did Alma of old: ''My soul was racked
with eternal torment; but I am snatched, and my soul is
pained no more'' (Mosiah 27:29).

Joy and Divine Love

Another indicator of a remission of sins often cited in the
scriptural conversion experiences is that of an overwhelming
feeling of joy. Alma contrasted this divine joy with his pains
of wickedness when he declared:

> And oh, what joy, and what marvelous light I did
> behold; yea, my soul was filled with joy as exceeding as
> was my pain!
> Yea, I say unto you, my son, that there could be
> nothing so exquisite and so bitter as were my pains.
> Yea, and again I say unto you, my son, that on the
> other hand, there can be nothing so exquisite and sweet
> as was my joy. (Alma 36:20–21.)

Another example of the joy that accompanies a remission
of sins is found in the miraculous conversion of King Lamoni
and his wife. After being taught the gospel by Ammon they
were ''overpowered by the Spirit'' and they all fell to the
ground ''as though they were dead'' (see Alma 19:13, 18).
Witnessing this remarkable scene, Abish, the converted
Lamanite woman, took the queen by the hand. The queen
arose and testified of her spiritual rebirth and declared: ''O
blessed Jesus, who has saved me from an awful hell!'' (Alma
19:29.) The record continues: ''And when she had said this,

she clasped her hands, being filled with joy" (Alma 19:30). The people of King Benjamin experienced something akin to that of Lamoni and his wife when they penitently petitioned God for his mercy and forgiveness. "Behold they had fallen to the earth, for the fear of the Lord had come upon them," the scriptures record. After the people had begged the Lord for forgiveness, the Spirit of the Lord came upon them, and they were filled with joy, having received a remission of their sins." (Mosiah 4:1, 3.)

Although we may not become so overwhelmed by the Spirit of the Lord that we fall to the earth in a spiritual trance, we can feel the "exquisite joy" that comes with a forgiveness of sins. Associated with this increased sense of joy is also an intensified awareness of divine love. Alma characterized this joyful feeling of love as a desire to "sing the song of redeeming love" (Alma 5:26). This in turn heightens our love, appreciation, respect, reverence, and awe for God. This intense love *for* God and *from* God, when coupled with the "exquisite joy" of forgiveness, causes us to declare with Nephi: "He hath filled me with his love, even unto the consuming of my flesh" (2 Nephi 4:21).

Moroni taught that "despair cometh because of iniquity" (Moroni 10:22). The darkness of despondency and discouragement is destroyed by the joy that accompanies a forgiveness of sins. A heart once heavy with hopelessness is lightened and illuminated by a hope instilled by the Comforter. "The remission of sins bringeth meekness, and lowliness of heart," declared Mormon, "and because of meekness and lowliness of heart cometh the visitation of the Holy Ghost, which Comforter filleth with hope and perfect love" (Moroni 8:26). Hope, humility, happiness, love, and light are all by-products of that divine type of joy that is promised to the repentant as the "baptism of fire" burns sin from their souls.

No Desire to Sin

Another important testament of the spiritual transformation that brings with it forgiveness for sins is a "mighty change" in our disposition and desires. King Benjamin's people experienced this "fruit of forgiveness" and joyfully declared: "The Spirit of the Lord Omnipotent . . . has wrought a mighty change in us, or in our hearts, that we have no more disposition to do evil, but to do good continually" (Mosiah 5:2). King Lamoni, his wife, and all those who on that occasion had been converted following Ammon's ministrations testified of the "mighty change" that took place in their lives when they were forgiven of their sins and spiritually reborn. "They did all declare unto the people the self-same thing—that their hearts had been changed; that they had no more desire to do evil" (Alma 19:33). Similarly, Alma spoke of the high priests whose "garments were washed white through the blood of the Lamb" and whose hearts and lives were changed by the sanctifying power of the Holy Ghost so that they "could not look upon sin save it were with abhorrence" (Alma 13:11–12).

Thus we can determine to a degree when we have been forgiven and to what extent we have been "born again" by examining our disposition toward evil and our desires to "do good continually." This condition does not mean that we never again succumb to any of the temptations surrounding us, but it does mean that sinfulness becomes repugnant to us and that our disposition is one of righteousness and doing good. As C. S. Lewis said, "What we *are* matters even more than what we *do*."[3] President Joseph F. Smith recounted his own experience and elaborated on the continuing application of this principle to all of us:

> The feeling that came upon me was that of pure peace, of love and of light. I felt in my soul that if I had sinned —and surely I was not without sin—that it had been forgiven me; that I was indeed cleansed from sin; my heart was touched, and I felt that I would not injure the smallest insect beneath my feet. *I felt as if I wanted to do good everywhere to everybody and to everything. I felt a newness of life, a newness of desire to do that which is right. There was not one particle of desire for evil left in my soul. . . .*

Oh! that I could have kept that same spirit, that same earnest desire in my heart every moment of my life from that day to this. Yet many of us who have received that witness, that new birth, that change of heart, while we may have erred in judgment or have made many mistakes, and often perhaps come short of the true standard in our lives, we have repented of the evil, and we have sought from time to time forgiveness at the hand of the Lord; so that until this day the same desire and purpose which pervaded our souls when we . . . received a remission of our sins, still holds possession of our hearts, and is still *the ruling sentiment and passion of our souls.*[4]

Love for Our Fellowmen

"I felt that I would not injure [even] the smallest insect beneath my feet," said President Joseph F. Smith in the previous statement. This attitude reflects another indicator of the "baptism with fire"—increased compassion for our fellowmen. King Benjamin stated it well when he explained to his people:

If ye have known of [God's] goodness and have tasted of his love, and have received a remission of your sins, which causeth such exceedingly great joy in your souls . . . ye will not have a mind to injure one another, but to live peaceably, and to render to every man according to that which is his due. . . . And also ye yourselves will succor those that stand in need of your succor; ye will administer of your substance unto him that standeth in need. (Mosiah 4:11, 13, 16.)

When we are forgiven of our sins and feel an intensified love and appreciation for the Lord, a natural outgrowth of those feelings is to desire that our fellowmen also experience the goodness and mercy of God. Enos exemplified this when, after the Lord had assured him that his sins were forgiven, his compassion and concern extended beyond self to his brethren, the Nephites, and even to his enemies, the Lamanites (see

Enos 1:9–13). From the time of Alma's miraculous conversion and the remission of his sins, he reported, "I have labored without ceasing, that I might bring souls unto repentance; that I might bring them to taste of the exceeding joy of which I did taste; that they might also be born of God, and be filled with the Holy Ghost" (Alma 36:24).

If we desire to know whether our repentance is accepted of the Lord it would be well for us to take inventory of our feelings of concern for others and our involvement in compassionate service to those around us. To what extent does our concern for the welfare of others correspond to that of the sons of Mosiah after they had been forgiven of their weighty transgressions? "Now they were desirous that salvation should be declared to every creature, for they could not bear that any human soul should perish; yea, even the very thoughts that any soul should endure endless torment did cause them to quake and tremble" (Mosiah 28:3).

Increased Spiritual Understanding

Several of the scriptural passages cited, as well as the statement from President Smith, include the word *light*. Sin causes us to become spiritually darkened, and a remission of sin removes that cloud and brings enlightenment. Thus another "fruit of forgiveness" is the renewed guidance of the Holy Ghost. This guidance not only brings comfort, peace, and joy, but also helps us to regain a spiritual perspective of life. President Wilford Woodruff testified of the increased spiritual discernment that accompanies a forgiveness of sins: "The veil of darkness, of doubt, and fear is taken from our minds, and we can see clearly where to go and what to do; and we feel that our spirit is right—that we are acceptable before the Lord our God, and are the subjects of his blessings.[5]

The Holy Ghost also teaches and testifies of the "mysteries of God" (see Alma 26:19–22). King Benjamin's people witnessed that accompanying the remission of their sins came "the manifestations of his Spirit" and "great views of that which is to come" (Mosiah 5:3). The Prophet Joseph Smith taught "the nearer man approaches perfection, the clearer are

his views."[6] President John Taylor also spoke of the increased
spiritual knowledge that only the penitent and pure can have;
he declared: "It has enlightened our minds, enlarged our un-
derstandings, extended our feelings, informed our judgment
—has warmed up our affections to God and holiness; has
nourished and cherished us, and put us in possession of principles that we know will abide for ever and for ever."[7]

Having the Image of God
Engraven upon Our Countenances

Each of us has perhaps known people whose spiritual
transformation from a life of wickedness to righteousness
produced such dramatic changes that their very appearance
and being was markedly different. Though hard to explain,
they actually possess an intangible but real and discernible
spiritual appearance that bespeaks a new life of goodness and
purity. Speaking to the Church in Zarahemla, Alma asked a
simple yet significant question to the Saints regarding their
level of spiritual rebirth or conversion. "Have ye received
[God's] image in your countenances?" (Alma 5:14.) Perhaps
Alma was referring to the literal, visible change that comes
upon a person whose sins are forgiven and whose life is re-
directed toward righteousness, but he probably was referring
also to the inward transformation of the whole being. As one
Latter-day Saint scholar of the scriptures explained:

> An "image" is not just an outward visual impression
> but also a vivid representation, a graphic display, or a
> total likeness of something. It is a person or thing very
> much like another, a copy or counterpart. Likewise,
> *countenance* does not simply mean a facial expression
> or visual appearance. The word comes from an old
> French term originally denoting "behavior," "de-
> meanor," or "conduct." In earlier times the word *coun-
> tenance* was used with these meanings in mind.
>   Therefore, to receive Christ's image in one's counte-
> nance means to acquire the Savior's likeness in behav-

ior, to be a copy or reflection of the Master's life. This is not possible without a mighty change in one's pattern of living. It requires, too, a change in feelings, attitudes, desires, and spiritual commitment.[8]

Determining whether we have been forgiven for our sins requires us to make a self-examination of our countenances. This self-examination is not conducted in front of any mortal mirror, but through sincere soul-searching and by listening to the still small voice. The Spirit of the Lord will help us to answer the question: Is our renewed commitment to follow the Savior discernible in our countenance, both in our *appearance* and, more important, in our *actions?* Sometimes we may recognize a remission of our sins as much by what we *do* as by what we *feel.* "If a man bringeth forth good works," declared Alma, "he hearkeneth unto the voice of the good shepherd" (Alma 5:41). We cannot perfect ourselves alone nor can we engrave the image of God upon our own countenances. It comes to us as we exercise faith in the Redeemer, repent of our sins, are forgiven, and continue to be "born again." Presumably without knowing of Alma's question, "Have ye received his image in your countenances?" C. S. Lewis made some good suggestions on that theme:

Christ, here and now, in that very room where you are saying your prayers, is doing things to you. It is not a question of a good man who died two thousand years ago. It is a living Man, still as much a man as you, and still as much God as He was when He created the world, really coming and interfering with your very self; killing the old natural self in you and replacing it with the kind of self He has. At first, only for moments. Then for longer periods. Finally, if all goes well, turning you permanently into a different sort of thing; into . . . a being which, in its own small way, has the same kind of life as God; which shares in His power, joy, knowledge and eternity.[9]

Becoming a "New Creature" in Christ:
Event or Process?

Most of the examples in the scriptures of men and women whose sins were forgiven and who experienced a spiritual rebirth involve dramatic or almost sensational events. Alma the Younger, Saul, Lamoni and his wife, and King Benjamin's people all underwent a sudden change of heart during a singular event or experience. But what about us? Will each of us experience this cleansing spiritual regeneration in the same manner? Elder Bruce R. McConkie answered:

> A person may get converted in a moment, miraculously . . . But that is not the way it happens with most people. With most people, conversion [and the accompanying remission of sins] is a process; and it goes step by step, degree by degree, level by level, from a lower state to a higher, from grace to grace, until the time that the individual is wholly turned to the cause of righteousness. Now this means that an individual overcomes one sin today and another sin tomorrow. He perfects his life in one field now, and in another field later on. And the process goes on until it is completed, until we become, literally, as the Book of Mormon says, saints of God instead of natural men.[10]

Sometimes this process is so gradual and subtle that we may be concerned that there has not been any significant spiritual change or that we cannot point to any single event or experience that told us we were forgiven. President Ezra Taft Benson explained that "most repentance does not involve sensational or dramatic changes, but rather is a step by step, steady and consistent movement toward godliness."[11] He further counseled us not to become discouraged by expecting the sensational or by comparing our experiences with those of others. "We must be careful, as we seek to become more and more godlike, that we do not become discouraged and lose hope. Becoming Christlike is a lifetime pursuit and very often involves growth and change that is slow, almost imperceptible."[12] The result is the same whether we are forgiven and become a "new creature" suddenly or gradually. As one doctrinal scholar observed:

> It seems unwise . . . to compare a seemingly unspectacular step-by-step *process* with someone's marvelous sudden *event,* and consider the process less valid. Both are valid ways to come to the baptism of fire. Though they do not happen in just the same way, the *results* are the same. The common elements are all there—forgiveness, peace of conscience, joy, spiritual enlightenment, desire for righteousness, commitment to obey, and responsibility. Perhaps the difference between these two approaches, i.e., the event vs. the process, can be likened to the difference between turning on a bright light in a dark room as opposed to watching the dawning of the day. The dawning is more gradual but results in just as much light.[13]

However this spiritual transformation comes to us, we need to continue to grow in gospel principles and be strengthened by the things of the Spirit. Being "born again" and forgiven of our sins does not mean that we have "arrived" at spiritual maturity, nor does it mean that we can never again lose those "fruits of forgiveness." President Harold B. Lee stated: "It is a possibility that one may be born of the Spirit and then, because of his sinfulness or slothfulness, he may lose the Spirit and fall from grace. The Spirit will not dwell in unholy tabernacles."[14] This important realization is reflected in the searching question posed by the prophet Alma, a question which we must continually ask ourselves: "If ye have experienced a change of heart, and if ye have felt to sing the song of redeeming love, I would ask, can ye feel so now?" (Alma 5:26.)

Forgiving Oneself

For many, a greater obstacle than receiving forgiveness from the Lord is receiving forgiveness from themselves. Unfortunately, some continue to punish themselves by carrying the unnecessary burden of past sins long after the Lord has forgiven them. Dwelling on past mistakes instead of looking forward with faith and a firm resolve stunts our spiritual growth and diminishes our ability to render substantive service in the kingdom of God. As someone once stated, "Trying to walk in the present, constantly looking over your shoulder at the past, can cause you to stumble over the future." Failure to forgive oneself indicates a *lack of understanding* of gospel principles and/or a *lack of faith* in the cleansing and healing power of the atonement of Jesus Christ. In the following statement Elder Richard G. Scott seems to sum up the problems with this type of continual self-punishment and recommends trust in the Savior as the solution.

> Can't you see that to continue to suffer for sins, when there has been proper repentance and forgiveness of the Lord, is not prompted by the Savior but by the master of deceit, whose goal has always been to bind and enslave the children of our Father in Heaven? Satan would encourage you to continue to relive the details of past mistakes, knowing that such thoughts make progress, growth, and service difficult to attain. It is as though Satan ties strings to the mind and body so that he can manipulate one like a puppet, discouraging personal achievement.
>
> I testify that Jesus Christ paid the price and satisfied the demands of justice for all who are obedient to His teachings. Thus, full forgiveness is granted, and the distressing effects of sin need no longer persist in one's life. Indeed, they *cannot persist* if one truly understands the meaning of Christ's atonement. . . .
>
> If you, through poor judgment, were to cover your shoes with mud, would you leave them that way? Of course not. You would cleanse and restore them. Would you then gather the residue of mud and place it in an envelope to show others the mistake that you made? No. Neither should you continue to relive forgiven sin. Every time such thoughts come into your

mind, turn your heart in gratitude to the Savior, who gave His life that we, through faith in Him and obedience to His teachings, can overcome transgression and conquer its depressing influence in our lives.[15]

Notes

1. Bruce R. McConkie, *A New Witness for the Articles of Faith* (Salt Lake City: Deseret Book Co., 1985), p. 239.

2. Harold B. Lee, "Stand Ye in Holy Places," *Ensign,* July 1973, p. 122; italics added.

3. C. S. Lewis, *Mere Christianity* (London: Collins Fount, 1960), p. 165.

4. Joseph F. Smith, *Gospel Doctrine* (Salt Lake City: Deseret Book Co., 1971), p. 96; italics added.

5. Wilford Woodruff, *Journal of Discourses,* 8:268.

6. Joseph Smith, *Teachings of the Prophet Joseph Smith,* p. 51.

7. John Taylor, *Journal of Discourses,* 7:318.

8. Andrew C. Skinner, "Alma's 'Pure Testimony,'" chapter 23 in *Studies in Scripture, vol. 7, 1 Nephi to Alma 29,* edited by Kent P. Jackson (Salt Lake City: Deseret Book Co., 1987), p. 301.

9. C. S. Lewis, *Mere Christianity,* p. 164.

10. Bruce R. McConkie, address at Brigham Young University First Stake Conference, 11 February 1968. (Cited in REL 231, "Doctrines of the Gospel," Student Study Guide, compiled by Larry E. Dahl and Brent L. Top, p. 150.)

11. Ezra Taft Benson, *The Teachings of Ezra Taft Benson* (Salt Lake City: Bookcraft, 1988), p. 71.

12. Ibid., p. 72.

13. Larry E. Dahl, "The Doctrine of Christ," in *The Book of Mormon: Second Nephi, the Doctrinal Structure*, edited by Monte S. Nyman and Charles D. Tate, Jr. (Provo, Utah: Religious Studies Center, Brigham Young University, 1989), p. 366.

14. Harold B. Lee, address to seminary and institute personnel, Brigham Young University, June 26, 1962.

15. Richard G. Scott, *Ensign,* May 1986, pp. 11–12.

8

Prevention Is Better than Redemption

One of the greatest blessings the gospel affords is the assurance that we can be forgiven of our sins through faith in the atoning blood of Christ. Some people, however, have a false sense of security based on their own narrow view of what repentance is and what it can and cannot do for us. This distorted view generates many misconceptions about the nature of repentance, the resultant effects of sin, and the availability of forgiveness. Some people actually believe that in some ways they are better off because they "sowed their wild oats." These people often feel that by virtue of their "experience" they may be better able to empathize with and help those who are struggling to repent of sin. Others may feel that they appreciate and understand the Atonement better by having been beneficiaries of its cleansing power. Still others claim that they could only have learned certain imperative lessons in the "hard knocks" school of sin.

These are all mistaken ideas about repentance. While we must continue to teach and testify of the glorious blessings associated with repentance, we cannot neglect the even greater blessings that flow from obedience and continued righteousness. "The more I see of life," stated President Harold B. Lee, "the more I am convinced that we must impress you young people with the awfulness of sin rather than to content ourselves with merely teaching the way of repentance."[1] Alma counselled his son Helaman:

> Teach them an everlasting hatred against sin and iniquity.
>
> Preach unto them repentance, and faith on the Lord Jesus Christ; teach them to humble themselves and to be meek and lowly in heart; teach them to withstand every temptation of the devil, with their faith on the Lord Jesus Christ.
>
> Teach them to never be weary of good works, but to be meek and lowly in heart; for such shall find rest to their souls.
>
> O, remember, my son, and learn wisdom in thy youth; yea, learn in thy youth to keep the commandments of God. (Alma 37:32–35.)

There are blessings and opportunities that steadfast faith, obedience, and good works afford us and which repentance and ultimate forgiveness may not ensure. For this reason, President Spencer W. Kimball declared: "Prevention is far better than redemption."[2] The blessings of obedience and rewards for righteousness are far better than the results of repeated repentance.

The Results of "Ritual Prodigalism"

One of the most subtle and successful tools of the adversary is to convince Latter-day Saints that since we are so abundantly blessed by the possibility of repentance, we have a spiritual safety net to catch us whenever we choose to fall. Sometimes this satanically inspired sentiment is characterized as "sowing your wild oats." "I can still repent" may be a true statement, but it is nonetheless shortsighted at best and damningly dangerous at worst. "Yes, one can repent of moral transgression," declared President Ezra Taft Benson. "The miracle of forgiveness is real, and true repentance is accepted of the Lord. But it is not pleasing to the Lord to sow one's wild oats . . . and then expect that planned confession and quick repentance will satisfy the Lord."[3] Elder Dean L. Larsen shared a personal experience he had with a young man which epitomizes this false sense of spiritual security that often results from misunderstanding the true nature of repentance:

> Not long ago I interviewed a young man who desired to fill a mission, but he had been guilty of some very serious transgressions during his teen years. . . . As we talked about his situation and the decisions he had made earlier in his life that led to his questionable standing in the Church, he said, "Oh, I knew that what I was doing was wrong, and I was sure that one day I would put things back in order and go on a mission."
>
> While I was pleased with this young man's desire to reorder his life and serve the Lord as a missionary, I was troubled by the apparent premeditated, calculated way in which he had allowed himself to move off the proper course to engage in some destructive, immoral behavior, and then, almost as if he were following a timetable set by himself, he had begun to reconstruct his resolve to be obedient.
>
> If my experience with this young man had been an isolated one, it would not be worthy of note here; unfortunately, however, it is not unique. There appears to be an increasing tendency and temptation for young people to sample the forbidden things of the world, not with the intent to embrace them permanently, but with the knowing decision to indulge in them momentarily as though they held a value of some kind too important or exciting to pass by. It is one of the great tests of our time.
>
> While many recover from these excursions into forbidden territory, an increasing number of tragedies are

occurring that reach out to bring a blight and a despair to many lives and that have long-lasting consequences. There is no such thing as private sin. Although its commission can be calculated . . . its effects cannot be regulated by the person guilty of the misbehavior. To believe otherwise is to become gullible to one of the most insidious lies ever perpetrated by the father of lies.[4]

A person who *plans* to go ahead and sin and then repent when he has had enough may find sincere repentance much more difficult than he imagined; this difficulty arises partly because he has had a calloused, manipulative view of the atonement of Jesus Christ. Moreover, if he repents to meet his own timetable (that is, for a mission, for temple marriage, etc.) rather than from genuine godly sorrow, he might think he has been forgiven when, in truth, forgiveness may elude him. This willful adventurism into the primrose paths of worldliness—with a predetermination to return to the "strait and narrow path"—was characterized by Elder Neal A. Maxwell as "ritual prodigalism."

> Why do some of our youth risk engaging in ritual prodigalism, intending to spend a season rebelling and acting out in Babylon and succumbing to that devilishly democratic "everybody does it"? Crowds cannot make right what God has declared to be wrong. Though planning to return later, many such stragglers find that alcohol, drugs, and pornography will not let go easily. Babylon does not give exit permits gladly. It is an ironic implementation of that ancient boast: "One soul shall not be lost." (Moses 4:1.)
>
> The philosophy of ritual prodigalism is "eat, drink, and be merry, . . . [and] God will beat us with a few stripes." This is a cynical and shallow view of God, of self, and of life. God never can justify us "in committing a little sin." (2 Ne. 28:8.) He is the God of the universe, not some night-court judge with whom we can haggle and plea bargain![5]

"Falling off the wagon"—to borrow a familiar phrase—whether such falls are frequent or few, premeditated or accidental, causes physical and emotional bumps and bruises that a hot, soapy bath and lots of linament cannot immediately or completely heal. Correspondingly, sinfulness—whether it be an extended relationship with worldliness or a brief flirtation with iniquity—has its own long-term consequences that may continue even after our "garments are made white in the blood of the Lamb." These long-lasting consequences include residual regret, loss of blessings and opportunities, and even the potential loss of the capacity to repent.

Residual Regret

Perhaps every person harbors in his heart, to some degree, an element of regret for past mistakes and a wish that he had never fallen prey to such temptations. Even though we may experience the peace of conscience and joy that accompanies a remission of sins, the memory of our sins does not necessarily leave us in this life. In fact, the more righteous we become, the more pained we may feel at our past foolishness. A former student in a religion class at BYU described this residual regret. This student granted permission for me to use his experience anonymously to help others realize that even repentance cannot wipe away all "side effects" of sin.

I have come to a personal awareness of the effects of the Atonement in my individual life, but it is a bittersweet awareness. I have learned that neither repentance nor forgiveness is free or simple. I rejoice greatly in the peace I have found. I know in a measure the feeling of having my guilt swept away and I am eternally grateful for the extent of the Savior's love for us. But I sorrow that this awareness came as it did.

Sin with the idea of repenting later is such an easy deception to fall into. In appearance you can have the world's fun and enjoyment. You can do the things you are commanded not to do, as long as you repent. And when you do repent—all is forgotten. But there are things lost that cannot be regained. After the process is complete (repenting and being forgiven) the guilt and pain are taken away, but regret remains—regret at hav-

ing sinned. I find for me that as my love and understanding of the Savior and his love increase, so does my
regret. I regret having knowingly done that which was
not right. I regret having wasted so much time and re-
versing the progression process. But more and more, I
have regret for the suffering that a loving Brother en-
dured, suffering for my sins, suffering because of my
selfishness.

Beyond regret—even in forgiveness, all is not restored as at first. When we sin against a greater light the
light in us is darkened and that kind of darkness stains
the mind and soul. It is easy to fall into a hole, and
even after you repent and are forgiven, you still have to
climb out, and that climb can be a long hard process.
The stains of darkness take a lot of scrubbing to completely remove.

Some people would imagine that you have to "taste
the bitter," or that certain experiences will make them a
better person. But sinning is full of deception, and
much of what a person "learns" must later be "un-
learned." . . .

Forgiveness is a wonderful reality and a glorious
hope. But nothing, no willful misuse of free agency for
momentary pleasure or the satisfaction of curiosity, can
compensate for that which is lost. Whether all can be
replaced eventually I don't know, but the process of
climbing back up where we were, the process of clean-
ing the "stains" of darkness (even after the darkness is
gone), the process of catching up to where you could
have been is a constant struggle, a great effort, and
takes time that could have been spent basking in a
greater light and a greater peace. You have to win
battles that were better off not fought.

Loss of Blessings and Opportunities

In addition to lingering pangs of regret, there are also
blessings and opportunities for service forfeited because of
our sinful departures from gospel principles. Even after re-

pentance, many of these blessings cannot be completely re-covered. A scriptural example of this is Esau. In his foolhard-iness, shortsightedness, and selfishness he sold his claim upon the birthright blessings to satisfy his physical appetite (see Genesis 27:34–38). Though he may have repented and may have been forgiven for his transgression, the inheritance was gone—given to another. Neither remorse nor reformation could reclaim the birthright for him. As the Apostle Paul wrote to the Hebrew Saints: "Lest there be any fornicator, or profane person, as Esau, who for one morsel of meat sold his birthright. For ye know how that afterward, when he would have inherited the blessing, he was rejected: for he found no place of repentance, though he sought it carefully with tears." (Hebrews 12:16–17.)

Prophets in this dispensation have likewise declared that some blessings lost through disobedience and rebellion are not regained even through repentance. President Joseph F. Smith declared:

Let me impress it upon you that one never can hold quite the same relation to a law of God which he has transgressed, as if one has lived in conformity with its requirements. It is unreasonable to expect it, and con-trary to the laws of nature to conclude that you can. If a person has determined that sin can easily be wiped out, and hence, that he will enjoy unlawful pleasures in youth, repenting in later life, with an idea in his mind that repentance will blot out completely the results of his sin and debauchery, and place him on a level with his fellow who has kept in virtue the commandments, from the beginning—time will wake him up to his serious and great mistake. He may and will be forgiven, if he repent; the blood of Christ will make him free, and will wash him clean, though his sins be as scarlet; *but all this will not return to him any loss sustained,* nor place him on an equal footing with his neighbor who has kept the commandments of the better law. *Nor will it place him in the position where he would have been, had he not committed wrong. He has lost something which can never be regained,* notwithstanding the perfection, the loving mercy, the kindness and forgiveness of the Lord God.[6]

Presidents Harold B. Lee and Spencer W. Kimball added their testimonies to that of President Joseph F. Smith and confirmed that one is never better off for having sinned. President Lee said:

> But now, please do not misunderstand the true meaning of the scriptures with respect to this matter. One may not wallow in the mire of filth and sin and conduct his life in a manner unlawful in the sight of God and then suppose that repentance will wipe out the effects of his sin and place him on the level he would have been on had he always lived a righteous and virtuous life. . . . The Lord extends loving mercy and kindness in forgiving you of the sins you commit against him or his work, *but he can never remove the results of the sin you have committed against yourselves by thus retarding your advancement toward your eternal goal.*[7]

President Kimball wrote: "God will forgive the repentant sinner who sins against divine law, but that forgiveness can never restore the losses he sustained during the period of his sinning."[8]

These inspired declarations should dispel the myth that living a life of sin and repenting later somehow makes us better or stronger. The Savior's greatness and expansive spiritual character was due to his righteousness, not to repentance. The Lord himself declared that blessings are predicated upon obedience (see D&C 130:18–19). We *lose* blessings through disobedience and sin and *gain* blessings through faithfulness and obedience.

Believing that sinning and eventual repentance yields significant spiritual "experience" or "knowledge" flies in the face of doctrinal reality. Groveling in the gutters of wickedness may make one "streetwise" to the ways of the world, but such "experience" does not compare to the "intelligence, or, in other words, light and truth" which is the "glory of God" (D&C 93:36). "A man is saved no faster than he gets knowledge," proclaimed the Prophet Joseph Smith, and he added: "As far as we degenerate from God, we descend to the devil and lose knowledge, and without knowledge we cannot be saved, and while our hearts are filled with evil, and we are studying evil, there is no room in our hearts for good, or studying good."[9] The kind of knowledge that brings salvation, opens up to us "the mysteries of the kingdom," and manifests the "power of godliness" (see D&C 84:19–23) is obtained by righteousness and purity, not by worldly experience.[10]

Feeling that we can better empathize with and better serve and strengthen the wayward because of our shared experiences is also a mistaken idea, however well-intended. Such empathy does not possess the same spiritual healing and lifting qualities that stem from charity—"the pure love of Christ"—a spiritual gift which God bestows upon "all who are true followers of his Son, Jesus Christ" (Moroni 7:47–48). The more righteous and obedient one is, the greater his compassion, his charity, and his capacity to "succor the weak, lift up the hands which hang down, and strengthen the feeble knees" (D&C 81:5).

Not only does sinning stunt spiritual growth and retard blessings but it also robs one of opportunities to serve and contribute. Just as Esau's birthright was gone forever, some sins cause us to lose irreversibly many of our opportunities to influence others and build the kingdom of God. A young man who has to get married as a consequence of his immorality may be forgiven of the Lord if he repents and may eventually be sealed in the temple, but he has lost the opportunities that could have come to him as a worthy young missionary. He may have other chances to serve and may even fill a full-time mission with his wife someday, but even those experiences cannot completely replace the lost opportunities of his earlier life. "Of course God is forgiving!" observed Elder Neal A. Maxwell. "But He knows the intents of our hearts. He also knows what good we might have done while AWOL."[11] We cannot go back and do the good we failed to do, anymore than we can *undo* all of the harm caused by our evil actions. As Elder Dean L. Larsen declared:

> The reverberations will affect the lives of those who indulge, as well as the lives of those who have loved and trusted them, in unfortunate and unforeseen ways for indefinite periods of time. As a consequence of these things, humanity slips inexorably to a lower level, the real power and influence in the Church and kingdom of God are diminished, and all mankind will inevitably feel the loss.[12]

Righteousness and continued obedience enlarge our capacities and expand our opportunities to contribute to the building of the kingdom. The good that can be done by those who continually cling to the iron rod and who are truly disciples for all seasons far surpasses the sporadic service of those who are merely summer soldiers. "What adventure in that great and spacious building would you trade," asked Bishop Glenn L. Pace of the Presiding Bishopric, "for the thrill and excitement of building the very kingdom the Savior will come to the earth to govern?"[13]

For those who have already strayed from the "strait and narrow" and lost blessings and opportunities they might have had, it is not too late. Do not focus on what you have lost; focus on what you may still accomplish. Sometimes repentant sinners work so diligently and steadily to make up lost ground that they may actually surpass those Saints who have never wandered far from the path but who have never "lengthened their stride" either.

Loss of Desire or Power to Repent

The Book of Mormon prophet Amulek cautioned against procrastinating the day of repentance, warning the people of the binding powers of sin. "For behold, if ye have procrastinated the day of your repentance . . . ," he warned, "ye have become subjected to the spirit of the devil, and he doth seal you his; therefore, the Spirit of the Lord hath withdrawn from you, and hath no place in you, and the devil hath all power over you" (Alma 34:35).

In the full context of his sermon, Amulek was speaking of the final state of the wicked "in that eternal world," but the "night of darkness" when Satan "doth seal you his"—surely that time referred to by Amulek can also occur in this life. Just as one's involvement in drug or alcohol abuse can result in a physical addiction, so persistent sinfulness, chronic disobedience, and willful rebellion can, if not checked through repentance, cause spiritual (as well as physical and emotional) "addiction" to sin. Elder Russell M. Nelson explained:

> From an initial experiment thought to be trivial, a vicious cycle may follow. From trial comes a habit. From habit comes dependence. From dependence comes addiction. Its grasp is so gradual. Enslaving shackles of habit are too small to be sensed until they are too strong to be broken. . . . Addiction surrenders later freedom to choose.[14]

Just as Elder Nelson referred to the "enslaving shackles of habit," the scriptures also portray Satan's temptations and powers as "awful chains" (2 Nephi 1:13), "chains of hell" (Alma 13:30), "bands of iniquity" (Mosiah 23:12), "bands of death" (Alma 5:7), and other images of spiritual bondage. While the Savior stands with arms of mercy open to us and beckons us to avail ourselves of his atonement, we must never cynically think that we can return to him whenever we like, for we may sadly discover what Amulek and two modern prophets cautioned against. "One of the greatest principles of the gospel of Jesus Christ is the principle of repentance," said President Harold B. Lee. "However, if one has sinned so seriously and becomes habitually a sinner, the spirit of repentance leaves, and he may or may not be able to repent."[15] Also, President Spencer W. Kimball declared:

> It is true that the great principle of repentance is always available, but for the wicked and rebellious there are serious reservations to this statement. For instance, *sin is intensely habit-forming and sometimes moves*

men to the tragic point of no return. Without repentance there can be no forgiveness, and without forgiveness all the blessings of eternity hang in jeopardy. As
the transgressor moves deeper and deeper in his sin,
and the error is entrenched more deeply and the will to
change is weakened, it becomes increasingly nearer
hopeless and he skids down and down until either he
does not want to climb back up or he has lost the
power to do so.[16]

How can we be sure that we will never reach that "tragic
point of no return"? How can those once shackled by sin but
now freed by forgiveness retain a remission of their sins and
continue their climb to greater spiritual heights? How can
those who have never veered far from the "strait and narrow" continue to cling to the "iron rod" though surrounded
by the "mists of darkness"? How can we avoid the regret and
loss of blessings and opportunities? Perhaps the answer to all
of these questions is found in the inspired words of President
Ezra Taft Benson: "It is better to *prepare and prevent* than it
is to *repair and repent*. The first line of defense . . . is to prepare ourselves to resist temptation and prevent ourselves
from falling into sin."[17]

Staying on the Lord's Side of the Line

The Apostle Paul taught the Corinthian Saints: "There
hath no temptation taken you but such as is common to man:
but God is faithful, who will not suffer you to be tempted
above that ye are able; but will with the temptation also make
a way to escape, that ye may be able to bear it" (1 Corinthians
10:13).

Unfortunately, some have construed this passage to mean
that one can never be tempted above one's ability to withstand. On the contrary, it is all too easy to allow ourselves to
get into situations in which we may actually lose the ability to
overcome the temptations we face. This is because we do not
avail ourselves of the "way to escape" that the Lord provides.

If we purposely or even inadvertently disregard the precautions and "escape routes" established by the Lord, we may indeed find ourselves tempted above and beyond our ability to withstand at that point. Alma's exhortation mirrors Paul's, but Alma clarifies the way in which the Lord makes "a way to escape" and tells us what we must do to be able to withstand.

> And now, my brethren, I wish from the inmost part of my heart, yea, with great anxiety even unto pain, that ye would hearken unto my words, and cast off your sins, and not procrastinate the day of your repentance.
>
> But that ye would humble yourselves before the Lord, and call on his holy name, and watch and pray continually, that ye may not be tempted above that which ye can bear, and thus be led by the Holy Spirit, becoming humble, meek, submissive, patient, full of love and all long-suffering;
>
> Having faith on the Lord; having a hope that ye shall receive eternal life; having the love of God always in your hearts (Alma 13:27–29).

Alma's words add important qualifications to Paul's promise. If we fail to "watch and pray continually" we can indeed "be tempted above that which [we] can bear." The resurrected Christ commanded the Nephites to "watch and pray always, lest ye be tempted by the devil, and ye be led away captive by him. . . . For Satan desireth to have you, that he may sift you as wheat." (3 Nephi 18:15, 18.) In our day and age the charge remains unchanged. "Pray always, that you may come off conqueror," the Lord admonished the Prophet Joseph Smith, "yea, that you may conquer Satan, and that you may escape the hands of the servants of Satan that do uphold his work" (D&C 10:5). President Ezra Taft Benson prophetically promised, "If you will earnestly seek guidance from your Heavenly Father, morning and evening, you will be given the strength to shun any temptation."[18]

While we continue to pray for strength to withstand temptation, we must also continue to follow King Benjamin's counsel: "Watch yourselves and your thoughts, and your words, and your deeds, and observe the commandments of God, and continue in the faith" (Mosiah 4:30). We must constantly be *watchful* as well as *prayerful* to ensure that our thoughts, words, and deeds stay in a spiritual "safe zone." President George Albert Smith spoke of the safety associated with keeping ourselves on "the Lord's side of the line":

> There are two influences in the world today, and have been from the beginning. One is an influence that is constructive, that radiates happiness and builds character. The other influence is one that destroys, turns men into demons, tears down and discourages. We are all susceptible to both. The one comes from our Heavenly Father, and the other comes from the source of evil that has been in the world from the beginning, seeking to bring about the destruction of the human family. . . .
>
> My grandfather used to say to his family, "There is a line of demarkation, well defined, between the Lord's territory and the devil's. If you will stay on the Lord's side of the line you will be under his influence and will have no desire to do wrong; but if you cross to the devil's side of the line one inch, you are in the tempter's power, and if he is successful, you will not be able to think or even reason properly, because you will have lost the Spirit of the Lord."
>
> When I have been tempted sometimes to do a certain thing, I have asked myself, "Which side of the line am I on?" If I determined to be on the safe side, the Lord's side, I would do the right thing every time. So when temptation comes, think prayerfully about your problem, and the influence of the Spirit of the Lord will enable you to decide wisely. There is safety for us only on the Lord's side of the line.
>
> If you want to be happy, remember, that all happiness worthy of the name is on the Lord's side of the line and all sorrow and disappointment is on the devil's side of the line.[19]

Notes

1. Harold B. Lee, *Decisions for Successful Living* (Salt Lake City: Deseret Book Co., 1973), p. 88.

2. Spencer W. Kimball, as quoted by Elder Paul H. Dunn, Conference Report, October 1977, p. 34.

3. Ezra Taft Benson, *The Teachings of Ezra Taft Benson* (Salt Lake City: Bookcraft, 1988), p. 70.

4. Dean L. Larsen, Conference Report, April 1983, p. 49.

5. Neal A. Maxwell, "Answer Me," *Ensign*, November 1988, p. 33.

6. Joseph F. Smith, *Gospel Doctrine* (Salt Lake City: Deseret Book Co., 1977), p. 374; italics added.

7. Harold B. Lee, *Decisions for Successful Living*, p. 100; italics added.

8. Spencer W. Kimball, *The Miracle of Forgiveness* (Salt Lake City: Bookcraft, 1969), p. 311.

9. Joseph Smith, *Teachings of the Prophet Joseph Smith*, compiled by Joseph Fielding Smith (Salt Lake City: Deseret Book Co., 1938), p. 217.

10. For an excellent discussion of how purity and keeping one's covenants brings about a knowledge of spiritual things, the reader should see Joseph Fielding McConkie, "The Spirit of Truth," in *To Be Learned Is Good If . . .* , edited by Robert L. Millet (Salt Lake City: Bookcraft, 1987), pp. 227–32.

11. Neal A. Maxwell, "Answer Me," *Ensign*, November 1988, p. 33.

12. Dean L. Larsen, Conference Report, October 1981, p. 37.

13. Glenn L. Pace, "They're Not Really Happy," *Ensign*, November 1987, p. 41.

14. Russell M. Nelson, "Addiction or Freedom," *Ensign*, November 1988, pp. 6–7.

15. Harold B. Lee, *Church News*, March 3, 1973, p. 4.

16. Spencer W. Kimball, *The Miracle of Forgiveness*, p. 117; italics added.

17. Ezra Taft Benson, "The Law of Chastity," address delivered at a Brigham Young University devotional, Tuesday, October 13, 1987.

18. Ezra Taft Benson, *The Teachings of Ezra Taft Benson*, p. 435.

19. George Albert Smith, *Sharing the Gospel with Others*, selected and compiled by Preston Nibley (Salt Lake City: Deseret Book Co., 1948), pp. 42–43.

9

"Press Forward with a Steadfastness in Christ"

However dedicated we may be in our desires and efforts to stay on the Lord's side of the line, all of us from time to time will fall prey to the temptations of the devil, stumble because of the weaknesses of the flesh, or slack off in our determination to serve the Lord. In fact, no person can become perfect in mortality. President Joseph Fielding Smith taught:

> Salvation does not come all at once; we are commanded to be perfect even as our Father in heaven is perfect. It will take us ages to accomplish this end, for there will be greater progress beyond the grave, and it will be there that the faithful will overcome all things, and receive all things, even the fulness of the Father's glory.
>
> I believe the Lord meant just what he said: that we should be perfect, as our Father in heaven is perfect. That will not come at once, but line upon line, and pre-

cept upon precept, example upon example, and even then not as long as we live in this mortal life, for we will have to go even beyond the grave before we reach that perfection and shall be like God.[1]

Repentance, therefore, is and will continue to be an ongoing process, not merely a series of events surrounding our sporadic seasons of sinning. Repentance involves a continual process of changing, growing, learning, becoming, and being. Like the Savior, we must receive "grace for grace"—living and learning the gospel "line upon line, precept upon precept" (see D&C 93:12–14).

The great, encouraging message of the gospel of repentance is that God does not often require sensational or extraordinary deeds of us but merely that we continually try to do a little better today than we did yesterday. He desires from us steady progress, not spurts of spirituality; firmness of resolve, not flashy but fleeting results. He is mindful as much of our desires, our determination, and our direction as he is of our deeds. "Worthiness is a process, and perfection is an eternal trek," declared Elder Marvin J. Ashton. "I am also convinced of the fact that the speed with which we head along the straight and narrow path isn't as important as the direction in which we are travelling. That direction, if it is leading toward eternal goals, is the all-important factor."[2]

King Benjamin likewise taught that retaining a remission of sins would be a continual process requiring a lifetime of "calling on the name of the Lord daily, and standing steadfastly in the faith," growing "in the knowledge of the glory of him that created you" (Mosiah 4:11–12). Elder B. H. Roberts explained that the simple things we do in life are those things that matter most in the ongoing repentance process that eventually leads to salvation.

> There is no one great thing that man can do and then do no more and obtain salvation. After entering into the kingdom of God, . . . it is by learning "precept upon precept; line upon line; here a little and there a little," that salvation will be made secure. *It is by resisting temptation today, overcoming a weakness tomor-*

row, *forsaking evil associations the next day, and thus day by day, month after month, year after year, pruning, restraining and weeding out that which is evil in the disposition, that the character is purged of its imperfections.* Salvation is a matter of character-building under the Gospel laws and ordinances, and more especially with the direct aid of the Holy Spirit.

Nor is it enough that one get rid of evil. He must do good. He must surround himself with circumstances congenial to the sensitive nature of the Holy Ghost, that he may not be offended, and withdraw himself; for if he does so, amen to the man's spiritual or moral development. He must cultivate noble sentiments by performing noble deeds—not great ones, necessarily, for opportunity to do what the world esteems great things, comes but seldom to men in the ordinary walks of life; but *noble deeds may be done every day; and every such deed performed with an eye single to the glory of God, draws one that much nearer into harmony with Deity.*[3]

When we feel disheartened—impatient that our progress is not as rapid as we expect, frustrated that we still succumb to temptations, or discouraged that we cannot seem to do all that we think we ought—the consoling words of Nephi can lift our spirits. Though Nephi lived on a high spiritual plane, he felt frustration occasioned by what he perceived as the weaknesses of the flesh; yet he understood the process and knew the source of strength needed for a steady journey.

Nevertheless, notwithstanding the great goodness of the Lord, in showing me his great and marvelous works, my heart exclaimeth: O wretched man that I am! Yea, my heart sorroweth because of my flesh; my soul grieveth because of mine iniquities.

I am encompassed about, because of the temptations and the sins which do so easily beset me.

And when I desire to rejoice, my heart groaneth because of my sins; nevertheless, I know in whom I have trusted.

My God hath been my support. . . .

He hath filled me with his love, even unto the consuming of my flesh. . . .

Awake, my soul! No longer droop in sin. Rejoice, O my heart, and give place no more for the enemy of my soul. . . .

Rejoice, O my heart, and cry unto the Lord, and say: O Lord, I will praise thee forever; yea, my soul will rejoice in thee, my God, and the rock of my salvation. . . .

O Lord, I have trusted in thee, and I will trust in thee forever. . . . I will lift up my voice unto thee; yea, I will cry unto thee, my God, the rock of my righteousness. Behold, my voice shall forever ascend up unto thee. (2 Nephi 4:17–21, 28, 30, 34–35.)

Even though we know that we can trust in the Lord, and even after we have felt of his mercy, we sometimes expect ourselves to be perfect in every aspect of our lives—right now. This unrealistic expectation may become an overwhelming burden that actually retards repentance and stifles spiritual progress. When we fall short of our preconceived notions of perfection (as we always will in this life), we tend to "browbeat" ourselves with undeserved self-criticism and guilt or to exhaust ourselves with unrealistic efforts to "work" our way to perfection. "What . . . can we do to manage these vexing feelings of inadequacy?" asked Elder Neal A. Maxwell. The insightful suggestions he gave in response to his own question are both helpful and hopeful:

We can distinguish more clearly between divine discontent and the devil's dissonance, between dissatisfaction with self and disdain for self. We need the first and must shun the second, for when conscience calls to us from the next ridge, it is not solely to scold but also to beckon.

We can contemplate how far we have already come in the climb along the pathway to perfection; it is usually much further than we acknowledge, and such reflections restore resolve. . . .

We can put our hand to the plow, looking neither back nor around, comparatively. Our opportunities as well as our gifts differ; some are more visible and impactful. . . .

We can make quiet but more honest inventories of our strengths. Most of us are dishonest bookkeepers and need confirming "outside auditors." He who in the first estate was thrust down delights in having us put ourselves down. Self-contempt is of Satan; there is none of it in heaven. We should, of course, learn from our mistakes, but without forever viewing the instant replays lest these become the game of life itself. . . .

We can . . . keep moving. Crosses are easier to carry when we keep moving. Men finally climbed Mount Everest, not by standing at its base in consuming awe, but by shouldering their packs and by placing one foot in front of the other. Feet are made to move forward.

We can know that when we have *truly* given what we have, it is like paying a full tithe; it is, in that respect, *all* that was asked. . . .

Finally, we can accept this stunning, irrevocable truth: Our Lord can lift us from deep despair and cradle us midst any care. We cannot tell Him *anything* about either aloneness or nearness.

This a gospel of grand expectations, but God's grace is sufficient for each of us if we remember that there are no *instant* Christians.[4]

As we strive to "keep moving" in our ongoing journey of repentance and obedience, though at times it may seem like climbing a spiritual Mount Everest, the words of King Benjamin seem especially appropriate. He cautioned: "And see that all these things are done in wisdom and order; for it is not requisite that a man should run faster than he has strength. And again, it is expedient that he should be diligent, that thereby he might win the prize; therefore, all things must be done in order" (Mosiah 4:27.) The Lord does not expect or want us to attempt to do more than we can—or more than that which is wise—but he desires that we diligently and steadily keep moving in the right direction. Doing our own personal best—whatever that may be—is doing "all we can do," which qualifies us to receive salvation through the grace of Jesus Christ (see 2 Nephi 25:23). Brigham Young declared:

> Those who do right, and seek the glory of the Father in heaven, *whether they can do little or much, if they do the very best they know how, they are perfect.* . . . "Be ye as perfect as ye can," for that is all we can do [though] it is written, "Be ye perfect as your Father who is in heaven is perfect." To be as perfect as we possibly can according to our knowledge is to be just as perfect as our Father in Heaven is. . . . *When we are doing as well as we know in the sphere, and station which we occupy here we are justified.* . . . We are as justified as the angels who are before the throne of God.[5]

Where do we go from here? What do we now need to do to be diligent and to do the best we know how? What remains in our ongoing repentance process? Nephi seems to summarize it best:

> Wherefore, ye must press forward with a steadfastness in Christ, having a perfect brightness of hope, and a love of God and of all men. Wherefore, if ye shall press forward, feasting upon the word of Christ, and endure to the end, behold, thus saith the Father: Ye shall have eternal life. (2 Nephi 31:20.)

I testify of the cleansing power of the blood of Christ. By virtue of his atoning sacrifice, if we abide the principles of his gospel which has been restored to the earth, we may experience the fulfillment of the Lord's promise to forgive our sins and "remember them no more" (see D&C 58:42). I have experienced in my own life the mercy and love of Jesus Christ and have witnessed the steady as well as the spectacular changes wrought in the lives of others through God's gift of repentance. Heavy hearts are lifted and sin-seared souls are miraculously healed by the Great Physician. Sins that are "as scarlet" can truly be as white as newly fallen snow.

May each of us continually partake of God's gift of repentance, being "steadfast and immovable, always abounding in good works," that we may come to know the blessing promised by King Benjamin (see Mosiah 5:15)

> that Christ, the Lord God Omnipotent, may seal you his, that you may be brought to heaven, that ye may have everlasting salvation and eternal life, through the wisdom, and power, and justice, and mercy of him who created all things, in heaven and in earth, who is God above all. Amen.

Notes

1. Joseph Fielding Smith, *Doctrines of Salvation*, compiled by Bruce R. McConkie, 3 vols. (Salt Lake City: Bookcraft, 1954–56), 2:18–19.

2. Elder Marvin J. Ashton, "On Being Worthy," *Ensign*, May 1989, pp. 20–21.

3. B. H. Roberts, *The Gospel and Man's Relationship to Deity* (Salt Lake City: Deseret Book Co., 1965), pp. 197–98.

4. Neal A. Maxwell, *Notwithstanding My Weakness* (Salt Lake City: Deseret Book Co., 1981), pp. 9–11.

5. Brigham Young, *Deseret News Weekly,* 31 August 1854, p. 37; italics added.

Index